THE HUMAN FACE OF MANAGEMENT

THE HUMAN FACE OF MANAGEMENT

▽

DOLF J.H. VAN DER HAVEN

За Ванка, защото си верен приятел който е олицетворението на съпричастие.

CONTENTS

9

10

Adding a book to the vast amount of Management literature seems like an effort that will largely go unnoticed. However, throughout the years of my managing large organisations, I developed methods that seem to be different from what other managers tend to do. This is not my own opinion, by the way, but purely based on feedback I received from people in my teams. The problem is that I never really understood why I did things differently. I believe I do now, though.

The problem with most Management books is that the basic ideas are all based on developments that took place in the 1970's. That was the era when psychologists developed an analytic view of people that fit behaviour into structures and patterns and favoured the purely rational over all other aspects of man (which are the physical, emotional and spiritual, as I will delve more into later). The notion that man can be explained in purely rational terms has never left Management theory and is the reason why I am very sceptical about what management training teaches. Not that I don't agree with most of it, but it is often an incomplete representation of what is really going on, especially when it comes to people management.

It was time to find out about the rest of what moved people and what moved companies (which, after all, consist of people), so I combined my varied background as a Geophysicist, a Network Engineer, a People Manager and a Psychotherapist into a new view of how I believe (people) management should be done.

This book consists of various chapters that I have written through the years. Some are based on the same principles as my previous book, The Healing Elephant, which is about psychotherapy. Other chapters do away with those principles again and base themselves on brand new insights. As a whole, I found out that there is a set of core subjects that my management philosophy is based on: Communication, Ecology and Attitude. These are the three cornerstones of not only my management style, but even of my life in general. As I wrote, it took me quite a while to find out about this, but age begets wisdom.

Communication is really where it all started for me: early in my career, I noticed that much in commercial companies broke down due to a lack of communication. People kept information to themselves instead of sharing it; higher management lost the connection with the people doing the work at the base of the company; organisations fell apart into silos, forming Chinese walls between departments that seemed impossible to break down, even though management paid lip service to having to do so. I then got fascinated with how communication should be working and coincidentally hit on something called Neuro-Linguistic Programming (NLP), which helped me a lot, but towards which I now have a more distant relationship, given that it suffers from the same 1970's rational focus that most Management theory suffers from as well. NLP does form a certain basis for the communication side of this book, though.

Ecology is to be understood in a very broad manner: it does not refer to taking care of the environment, but has a much broader and general definition. Ecology means making sure that what you do does not harm yourself, others or the environment or context in which we are acting. Ecology can in this sense also be translated as "Ethics" if interpreted in a broad sense. Ethics itself is a largely misunderstood part of running a business, as it is most often merely associated with compliance, following the rules. Ethics goes far beyond that, though, and becomes a cornerstone of the manager's behaviour and attitude once properly understood.

Attitude, then, is another aspect that mystified me since my training as a psychotherapist (something I started doing halfway my career as a result of being fascinated with communication). In The Healing Elephant, I wrote about the attitude that is appropriate for a therapist towards his clients. I have since then applied the same principles to my job as a manager and this resulted in a more concrete idea about attitude, paired with Ethics, which becomes universally applicable in any profession and context.

Finally, none of this would have been possible to conceive as an integral whole without the profound influence of the work of Ken Wilber. He is also someone whose ideas need to be taken with caution and a grain of salt here and there, but the principles of his Integral Model, which I will explain in the first chapter, are still something that I am convinced of as a highly useful model of the world that can be applied in many different situations.

ACKNOWLEDGEMENTS

Thanks are mainly due to all my colleagues throughout the years, for enduring me and my managerial style. In particular, though, two people among them need to be mentioned explicitly. Thanks to Kim Blom for first having confronted me with the ethical ramifications of being the manager of a close friend and (re-)opening up new worlds to me. Ivan Raychinov I thank for proof-reading this book and trying to make sense of it, but foremost for being the embodiment of Empathy, simply by being himself and being one of the greatest friends I'll ever have.

Specifically for the chapter about Talent Management, thanks are due to the following people: my own High Potentials, Kim Blom, Matthew Taylor, Rob Jansen, Hamid Abbou and Gustavo Firmino. Initial suggestions came from Charles Liem at Abbott Laboratories.

Finally, I have gratefully used input from Karin van der Haven at Nike and from Ido Shikma and Erica van Wingen at CGI.

Most of all, thanks is due to Charles Liem, for always being there for me.

This chapter is the only purely theoretical one, so bite through it – I'll keep it as light as possible.

The Integral Model that will be introduced in this chapter is based on the model that was developed by Ken Wilber, an American thinker who has read written a lot in areas such as psychology, philosophy and spirituality. This is the only chapter that is purely theoretical, but I need to go through it with you in order to show the basis from which the rest of the chapters derive their more practical contents.

Very briefly summarised, the Integral Model basically divides the world and every phenomenon in it into four parts that he calls Quadrants. Furthermore, he combines this division with a general hierarchical model of levels of development in each of the quadrants. The purpose of this model is to show how a person's or group's current state (level of development) in a particular area (quadrant) can or needs to be related to other areas and states that are seemingly nothing to do with the former.

THE FOUR QUADRANTS

The four quadrants are the basis of the Integral Model of Ken Wilber's. The quadrants make a division in the way in which all things, living beings and events in the world can be seen by us. The object of what is seen can be anything: the model includes man himself, politics, medical science, economics, culture, etc. Also, the way in which things are seen can be any way. Each of the quadrants forms a specific perspective on things, so a way in which you can look at something.

Let's make this more concrete and more visual. As you can see in the figure below, Wilber's model makes a division of the world in two ways. The first division (the one shown on the right hand side, dividing between an upper part and a lower part) is between the individual, a single person such as an employee or a manager, and the collective, the greater group that this person is part of, such as a team, a company or society as a whole. The second division (the one shown on the left, dividing between a left hand side and a right hand side) is that between an internal view on things and an external view on things. The internal view is the experience of a person or a group itself, their outlook on things. This includes thoughts, emotions, cultural views, etc. The external view is that of an observer of that person or that group, how they are looked at from the outside. This looks at things like behaviour, structure of an organisation and interaction between people.

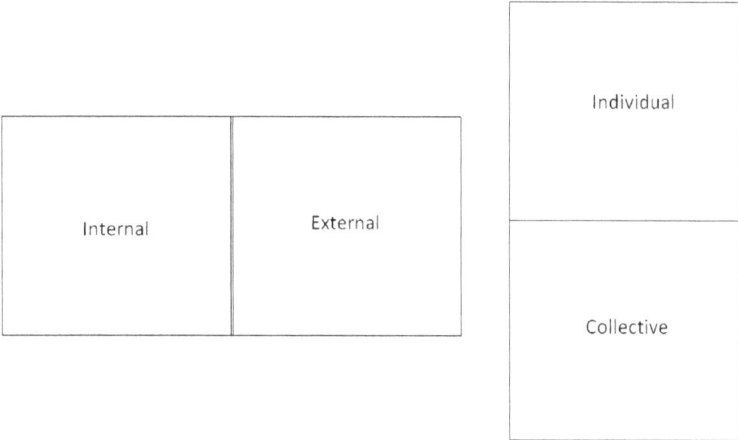

Individual
Internal	External
Collective

Two divisions of the world: Internal versus External and Individual versus Collective (after Ken Wilber).

So with this, we have a division between the individual and the collective and a division between the internal perspective and the external perspective. If we now put these two divisions together and on top of each other, we get the four quadrants:
- The **internal** experience of the **individual** (internal-individual, upper left quadrant),
- The **external** vision on the **individual** (external-individual, upper right quadrant),
- The **internal** experience of the **collective** (internal-collective, lower left quadrant) and
- The **external** vision on the **collective** (external-collective, lower right quadrant).

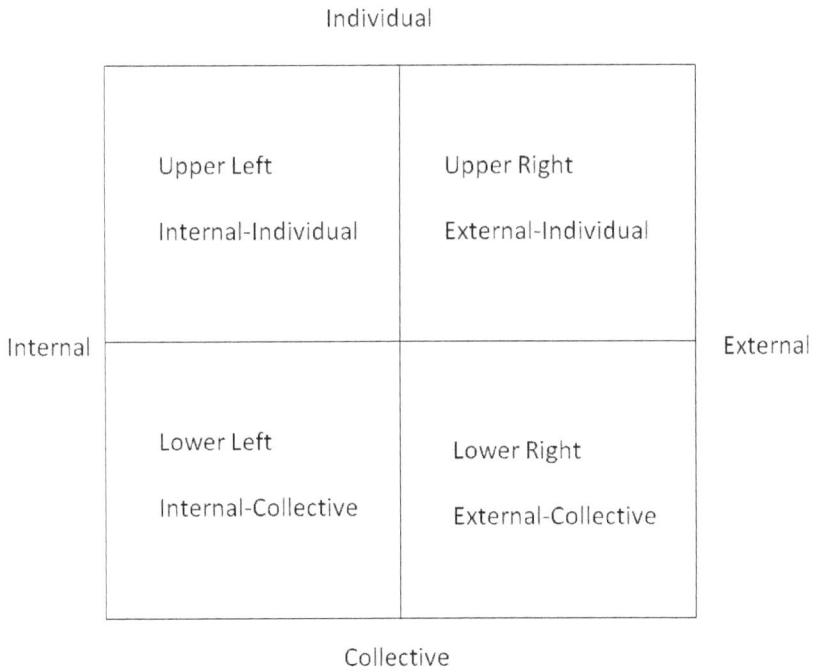

Individual

Upper Left Internal-Individual	Upper Right External-Individual
Lower Left Internal-Collective	Lower Right External-Collective

Internal — External

Collective

The four quadrants (after Ken Wilber)

This is probably still pretty abstract, so it is time to clarify it with something more concrete. If we apply these theoretical divisions on a person working for a company, then we can give the following contents to each of the quadrants.

The Upper Left (UL) quadrant deals with the internal-individual aspects of man, that is, the personal experience of someone about his life and what happens in it. The psychology of this person is in this quadrant as well as his personal development in the mental, emotional, psychological and spiritual areas. What is his general attitude at work, how does he feel about his job, does he have enough knowledge to do his daily assignments?

The Upper Right (UR) quadrant deals with the external-individual aspects of the employee: the development of the body, including the brains. Also classical medical science and behaviour are part of this quadrant. It deals with how man is seen from the outside. How does the employee behave at work? What impact does a possible health situation have on his job? Is he physically fit to do the work that is asked from him?

The Lower Left (LL) quadrant is the internal-collective or the experience of a group of people: a family, a society and in the management context, a team or company. Similarly to how an individual employee has emotional, cognitive and spiritual experiences of himself, a team has similar experiences. How does the team fit together? How do they look at other teams? What team-culture exists and how does that culture fit into the overall corporate culture? Is there good communication between team members?

Finally, we have the Lower Right (LR) quadrant. This is the external-collective side of things, in which a group of people is looked at from the outside. So it mainly deals with the structure of that group and how the people in that group deal with each other. What is the political climate in the company? Is a hierarchical structure the right one for the company or should it be flatter or cell-based? How is the interaction between departments?

The quadrants are not totally independent or isolated, but all of them are connected to each other: there are no walls between the quadrants, there rather are connections and interactions between different aspects from two or more quadrants that each deal with a part of a person. For example: the work attitude of an employee (that exists in the upper left quadrant) has a relationship with his behaviour (that exists in the upper right quadrant): behaviour is the expression of this attitude. This work-attitude and that of others in the team also lead to a certain way of thinking within that organisation that these employees are part of (in the lower left quadrant). That way of thinking in that organisation has in its turn an influence on how the interaction between people of that team is formed (in the lower right quadrant). It is useful to be able to see these relationships between the quadrants, so as to be able to get a full view of a situation, a problem or a human being. Having this full view of all perspectives from the four quadrants is referred to as having an Integral (all-encompassing) perspective.
But there is more to that: we are now going to add development to all quadrants.

LEVELS OF DEVELOPMENT

It has been found that people go through a number of stages or levels of development in many aspects of who they are. This development can be in the areas of their psychology, knowledge, needs and other aspects. Maslow's hierarchy of needs for instance, shows a development of the individual needs of a person going from basic Physiological to Safety, Love and Belonging, Esteem up until Self-actualisation. These levels exist according to the Integral Model within the upper left quadrant, which after all deals with the individual internal features.

19

The two other quadrants, however, have levels of development as well, although these may not be equally apparent at first glance.

The upper right quadrant, which deals with the external personal development, has a development chain that goes from atoms to molecules (in which there are atoms), to cells (in which there are molecules), to the body (in which there are cells). This is another hierarchical development model, now applied to the external side of man, similar to how the psychological development models are applied to the internal experience. Similarly, ask a colleague how she feels today, rating her health between 1 and 10. The answer indicates a number of levels of well-being in an external, physical manner.

The lower left quadrant, the one of the internal development of a group, knows a hierarchy of cultural development. That development has been described in terms of levels that succeed each other: from archaic to magic to mythic to rational to reflective to globalist. These expressions indicate in how far cultures are inclusive of people and of other cultures and how they explain events happening in the world.

The lower right quadrant, in which the development of societies is described, knows a development of these groups in the following manner: from tribes to hunters-gatherers to horticulturists to agriculturists to industrial nations to worldwide information networks. These names indicate how societies have grown to ever more complex structures requiring more and more information to function well.

Just as with personal development, here we have another three examples of hierarchical development models. And it turns out that all these models of development have a characteristic in common, namely they are *holonic*: higher levels *transcend* lower levels and *include* them. This means that higher levels of development go beyond the lower levels (i.e. transcend) in terms of how they function and how complex they are. But it also means that the higher levels don't just drop the functions of the lower levels: they include those functions and make them part of the greater complexity of the higher level. The higher levels can therefore not exist without the lower levels, because they would otherwise miss the foundation they were built on.

Similarly to why the four quadrants cannot be independent of each other but influence each other, these four examples of development models cannot be separate from each other. For instance, a company that develops itself from a basic start-up without any management structure to a large industrial organisation (forms of development in the lower right quadrant) needs a supporting cultural change from magic or mythic to rational or reflective (forms of development in the lower left quadrant). That cultural change can only happen if the individual people in that culture change themselves along with the organisation (in the upper left quadrant). And someone who develops himself personally, not only does so internally, but also externally in the sense that cognitive functions of the brains develop themselves (in the upper right quadrant). All these ways of development are therefore in fact closely related to each other and form one and the same development, albeit that this development can be expressed in four different quadrants.

This last fact points to an important part of the Integral Model: even though the various aspects of people are described with different terminology and with different models, each of those still describe only one single aspect of a phenomenon. However, that same phenomenon always expresses itself in all four quadrants. Seen from the perspectives of those quadrants, that phenomenon can be described in four different ways, but in the end, only a combination of those four descriptions provides a full view of it. It is that full, or Integral, view that we are looking for in order to be able to see the whole picture of people and the society or companies they are part of.

By combining the Integral Model and its four quadrants with models of development in all those quadrants, we can get a full Integral Model. This model can be depicted as in the following figure:

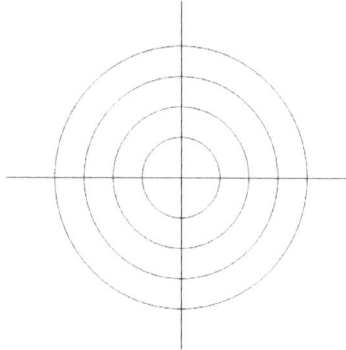

The complete Integral Model: the four quadrants and a model of development.

Development is shown as a number of concentric circles that transcend and include each other. On top of that, the four quadrants are shown, resulting in a full Integral Model of interrelated development in four perspectives on the world. This integration of the four quadrants and the development model is also referred to as "All Quadrants, All Levels" or AQAL. The AQAL model gives a description of a phenomenon from the perspectives of an individual person and the community that he is part of, both from an internal and from an external perspective. It is this AQAL or Integral Model that I will be using to explain the way of working of Integral Therapy.

To summarise: the idea behind the Integral Model with the four quadrants is the fact, that a phenomenon and, specifically in the context of this book, an employee or a manager in a company, can only be fully understood and managed if aspects from all four quadrants are taken into account. The internal experience, the external state and behaviour, the culture that someone is part of or comes from and the social structure of the organisation he works in. All these perspectives have their influence on people.

Let's now have a look at what this model means when we are talking about Management.

2. WORKPLACE ETHICS

Ethics are boring – or so I hear from colleagues who need to do yet another compliance-training. Ethics is much more than just making sure people follow the rules, though. This chapter aims at widening the scope of traditional company ethics and show that real ethics are far wider-reaching than what is sold in compliance-training courses.

Since the discovery of several bookkeeping scandals a couple of years ago, the need was found for better ethical practices in companies. This not only resulted in legislation being passed to enforce practical standards (e.g. the Sarbanes-Oxley Act), but also the creation of more awareness among the employees of these companies about ethical issues. Companies created Codes of Conduct (COCs), founded Ethics Boards and employees went through extensive training sessions in order to increase their awareness of ethics. However, looking at the contents of such "ethics" courses, COCs and procedures surrounding Ethics Boards, the impression is invariably that the word "Ethics" is interpreted in a very limited way, focussed merely on *compliance* with rules that are either externally imposed (e.g. Laws) or adopted by the companies themselves (e.g. COCs). In reality, ethics is something much broader and deeper than that and the implications of the full definition of ethics in the workplace is worth looking at if a company wants to be ready for real ethical governance. The aim of this chapter is therefore to present a more comprehensive model of ethics and apply that model to practical workplace situations. This model of ethics builds on the Integral Model that we introduced in the previous chapter and applies it to the field of ethics and morality. This will be followed shortly by a number of practical examples of how the model can be applied in the workplace.

For starters, the model of Integral Ethics will be introduced that is helpful in order to look at a phenomenon from all perspectives that are needed. After this, the model will be used to determine what the various aspects of ethics are that we need to take into account. Then, these aspects are used to fully define workplace ethics and the practical application thereof.

APPLICATION OF THE INTEGRAL MODEL TO ETHICS

LEVELS OF ETHICS

Personal development means that we grow in certain aspects of who we are, such as mentally, physically, emotionally, but also in terms of our own ethics or morality. Growth typically means that more and more of the world around us gets included in our view on things. In the field of ethics, the question is, who do we include in our consideration of an issue? Whose interests do we look at when making a decision? Is it just our own interests or the interests of our families, our company, or our nation? Just like other aspects of life, Ethical development can be divided in a number of levels that succeed each other and, in a simplified scheme, look as follows.

Level	Scope of Ethical View
Multi-world Centric, Pluralistic	All beings, pluralistic
Post-conventional, World centric	All human beings, All of us
Conventional, Ethnocentric	Us, team, family, nation
Pre-conventional, Egocentric	Me

Levels of ethics.

These stages or levels are in integral theory said to "transcend and include" each other, meaning that higher levels transcend, but also include all lower levels. This means that higher levels

25

encompass more of the world around us and include the views of the preceding levels. So the lower levels do not disappear when we grow, but will always be present as the foundation on which the higher levels rest. These stages can be depicted as concentric circles, indicating the "transcend and include" nature of them: lower stages are circles closer to the centre; higher stages are larger circles, encompassing the circles of the lower stages. As you can see in the previous table, the basic stage in the field of ethics is an *egocentric* one, where the only interest of a person is him or herself. This is a person who does not care about others or the world around him, as long as his own views are honoured and his interests take precedence. The next level is the *ethnocentric* one, where the smaller or larger group that one is part of is included in the scope of interest. This can be as small as a partner, or be extended to the team, the company or the nation. Here, the interests of the smaller group, such as the own team or company, need to take precedence, if necessary at the cost of other teams, the environment or other companies. The *world-centric* level is next, where all human beings are taken into account in ethical decisions. So not only the people working for the company, but also external stakeholders, such as people living near your factory, suppliers and consumers. The last level, for the purpose of this paper, is the Multi-world Centric or *Pluralistic* level, where all living beings, human or not, are included. Here, developments such as Corporate Social Responsibility (CSR) enter the consciousness of companies, taking care of more than just the company's interests, but also involving the external community, the environment and the world in general.

The stages of ethics can also be named slightly differently, based on what is considered "conventional." The *Conventional* stage of ethics then reflects an attitude that strictly adheres to the rules of the group, to social norms and traditions. There are absolute distinctions between right and wrong. Before this stage, there is the *pre-conventional* one, which is a stage in which these rules are not deemed important from an egocentric point of view. This stage rejects those rules that are not considered favourable for the individual. On the other hand, the stages beyond the conventional one are called *post-conventional* and these reject the conventional rules and traditions as well, but from a different point of view: traditions are said to prevent personal development and are being replaced with individual norms and rules that are considered more appropriate for the development of all people. This is different from the pre-conventional stage, as that one is based on egocentric motives that reject any external rules and this one is based on world-centric intentions that promote better-tailored, individual rules.

In practical terms of human behaviour, note that for people functioning at different levels of development, their ethical choices may be totally different if they were put in the same situation. For instance, when negotiating a deal with a customer, is the interest of the *individual* negotiator the only thing taken into account (e.g. his own sales target) or the interests of the company (e.g. overall revenue and profit)? Are in agreeing internal processes only the interests of your own team important, or also the interests of the other teams that are involved? How about the interests of the company as a whole? How about the interests of the company and the customer together? This shows how greater inclusion of involved people makes decision-making and specifically ethical decision-making more complex.

ETHICS IN MULTIPLE QUADRANTS

Apart from the developmental levels, ethics can also be looked at from the four quadrants or perspectives that were described before. If you take the Integral Model introduced in chapter 1 and in each quadrant look at ethics, you get the following results.

Morality	Behaviour
Ethics	Laws

Ethics in the AQAL Model

These expressions seem to be the same, but the way in which I will be using them is subtly different. The individual expressions can be explained as follows.

Morality includes our personal intentions, promises and commitments. It is based on our internal experience of what is right and what is wrong. This internal experience is primarily based on our development in other areas, such as cognition, conscience and Self-Reflection. In this quadrant, we make our own determination of what is important to take into account when making ethical decisions. Our personal moral virtues, beliefs and values play a significant role in these decisions.

Behaviour refers to the external activities that result from our morality. The actions we take based on our morality reflect the practical results of our ethical decisions. Note that not only does morality influence our actions, but our actions also provide feedback for our morality. Once the result of our actions is known, we can morally assess whether our actions were justified or not. This may result in us developing our morality further, based on that feedback. This quadrant also permits us to have a neutral look at the situation that we are in and observe our actions and those of others objectively.

Ethics is the equivalent of morality applied in a group context. Within organisations, there is a commonly understood set of moral standards that members of the organisation are expected to adhere to. These standards are often not written down, but implicitly applied. For instance, not using office supplies for private purposes is a generally understood rule in many companies that is, however, not always explicitly written down in Codes of Conduct and the likes. Relationships with other people in the company and with customers are in this quadrant, for which it should be verified how these are affected by our decisions and actions. Apart from relationships, also culture, religion, gender, etc. are to be considered here.

Laws are the external rules imposed on organisations. Organisations are expected to adhere to the laws and regulations that apply to them and need to base their conduct and internal processes on them. When looking at Codes of Conduct of several companies, these are usually written somewhere in between this quadrant, i.e. adherence to the law, and the lower left quadrant, i.e. the company's own ethics.

ALL-QUADRANTS, ALL-LEVELS (AQAL) ETHICS

We are going to do the same trick as we did in chapter 1 now, combining the four quadrants with the various levels of development that exist in them. Then, if we take the view of ethics at all levels and in all quadrants, we arrive at a comprehensive view of ethics that can be called "Integral Ethics" or "AQAL Ethics."

So what is it that is central in Integral Ethics? In the first place, it looks at *depth* and *span*. (Vertical) depth is defined as the level of care and compassion we have for other beings, equivalent to the levels defined before. The greater the depth, the more levels we take into account in our ethical decisions. (Horizontal) span is the responsibility we take in the quadrants: the more quadrants we take into account, the greater the span. Integral Ethics protects and promotes the greatest depth and the greatest span and that is the central point of view that we will be taking in the practical examples that follow. This means that the view that comes from a higher ethical level and includes the greatest community takes precedence over lower ethical levels, because it is more developed and more inclusive than views with lower depths. At the same time it says that we need to look at ethical dilemmas from all four quadrants: our own internal and external aspects and our company's, society's or even greater group's internal and external aspects. So views with a greater span are more important than views with lower spans, because if the number of perspectives taken into account.

Taken together, views can have a sum of span and depth that determines the overall ethical development of that view.

Apart from this, three *values* need to be taken into account as well: Ground Value, Intrinsic Value and Relative Value. These are related to the value we attach to living beings around us and what we believe constitutes that value. These three values are defined as follows.

Ground Value: every being is *equally* deserving of ethical regard. This means that whatever the nature of a being, be it a dog, a child or a grown-up human being, the ground value is the same and therefore every being deserves to be valued in the same way.

Intrinsic Value: the more *developmental* depth a being has, the more its intrinsic value is. This makes a differentiation between the dog, the child and the grown-up in terms of this specific value: the dog has a lower intrinsic value than the child and the child has a lower intrinsic value than the grown-up. This may have an implication in specific ethical circumstances.

Relative Value: this refers to the *usefulness* of beings in specific contexts. This third value looks at the practical use of someone in a certain situation. For example, in an extreme case where a group of people needs to survive in the mountains and for some reason need to reduce their team size, who is most useful to keep in the group, the seasoned mountaineer or the accountant? It can be said that the account has in this case a lower relative value than the seasoned mountaineer.

PUTTING INTEGRAL ETHICS INTO PRACTICE

Now that all the elements of ethics from an integral framework have been described, let's look at how we can put this into practice in the workplace. This will be a two-fold discussion: in the first place, the question should be answered how you put ethics into practice and after that, a number of practical examples will be dealt with that should be recognisable to many readers.

THE PRACTICE OF INTEGRAL ETHICS

In practice, Integral Ethics should be asking a number of relevant questions for each dilemma we find ourselves in. These questions should at least cover each of the four quadrants and in those quadrants should be considered at several ethical levels. In this way we should be able to cover both the full depth and the complete span of ethics. In what follows, the personal decisions taken based on the upper left quadrant's morality are contrasted with and supplemented by the input we get from the other quadrants.

Making a seemingly easy start with this approach, let's look at the lower right quadrant, in which the laws of society are located. The most basic question when dealing with an ethical situation is obviously if there are any laws that are broken by our decisions. But this question cannot be looked at in isolation. It would be easy to base our ethical decisions on external laws only, but what if our own morality or our group's ethics are in conflict with the applicable laws? You need to realise that laws are a reflection of the society they are defined in and as such laws can exist at various levels of development. If the laws that apply to our society are defined at a lower level than the one we function at (i.e. in this case society has a shallower depth than we do), then we should determine if our moral or ethical standards need to overrule those laws. For instance, some Arab countries require foreign companies to sign non-Jew declarations for employees that want to work in those countries. If those requirements are part of the local law, looking from the lower right quadrant, we'd need to sign such a declaration. However, when we look at it from the point of view of our personal morality or our company's ethics, we could decide that signing such a declaration is in conflict with those higher standards and can therefore not be done. The consequences would then possibly be the loss of our business in those countries, which needs to be balanced against the ethical dilemma. Is it more important to win this business or is it more important to stick with our ethical principles? This is to do with the beliefs and values we hold, about which more will be said in a later chapter. Staying in the lower right quadrant, we know that the ethics of the group need to be taken into account. Limiting the group to mean the company in this case, we find a subtle interaction between the individual morality in the upper left quadrant and the company's ethics in the lower left quadrant. Company ethics are usually imposed onto the employees via Codes of Conduct or similar documents, which in turn are often mainly based on (lower right) laws and regulations and the intention to adhere to them. Often, externally-imposed laws and regulations are translated into company standards that provide black-and-white guidelines for the employees' behaviour. In that sense, the so-called company ethics actually constitute a move of the company's ethical views in the lower left quadrant to the applicable laws in the lower right quadrant.

The lower left quadrant is more involved with shared values and beliefs, corporate culture and internal and external communication. These can be found back in some Codes of

Conduct and in that case show something of the ethical level at which the company functions. It won't be surprising that this level is often the conventional, ethnocentric level at which the focus is on following the rules and taking care of the interests of the company and directly connected external parties such as customers and suppliers. Within a company, there may be an apparent conflict between an employee's morality (upper left) and the company's ethics (lower left). It is the conflict between notions of "What is right?" from a personal perspective and "what is right?" from a company's perspective. This conflict may seem tough to deal with, but can actually be looked at in a less complex way using levels of ethics. First, it needs to be acknowledged that the ethics of the company may be at a different (lower or higher) level than the morality of the individual employee. Then, from the point of view of Integral Ethics' strive for the greatest depth and the greatest span, it should be acknowledged that in most cases the interests of the company as a whole transcend the interests of the individual. This is the case in ethical situations that affect the whole company or the team that the employee is part of, but not in cases that only affect the individual employee. For instance, a pharmaceutical company may require all employees to report on accidents in order to safeguard the employees' safety by monitoring potential hazards and taking corrective action before serious accidents happen. An individual employee whose lab setup exploded but was not injured may think that it is not necessary to report this incident given that he was not harmed. However, the company requirement is there for the purpose of safeguarding the greater community and as such is ethically a level higher than the employee's morality. On the other hand, a conflict between an individual employee who, for example, has missed a promotion, whereas others with a similar track record did get their promotions, has a case that may be a conflict between the individual's sense of fairness and the company's sense of fairness. If no agreement can be found in these kinds of cases, the employee may want to consider the question whether a company with ethical standards that are below his own standards is the right place for him to work at. Following your own ethical standards may have to result in leaving a place where those standards are not honoured.

To complete the cycle through the quadrants, the upper right quadrant deals with the individual behaviour; this necessarily is a result of a balance between aspects from the other three quadrants. Our behaviour is the result of ethical decisions we make based on external laws and rules, the team's, the company's or society's ethics as part of their culture and our own personal sense of morality. Balancing the feedback we get from each of these on an ethical decision we need to make results in an action we take and as such reflects in our behaviour. Seen from the other side, our behaviour shows the decisions we, consciously or not, made in an ethical sense. Say a sales representative approaches his customers in an overly informal way, which is perceived by the customers as lacking respect. This behaviour probably is not in violation with any laws. The customer may think this may be a reflection of the company's culture, though, and therefore condoned by the company's ethics. However, it may merely be a reflection of the individual sales rep's morality and therefore in violation with the ethical standards of the company. A response to potentially complaining customers may have to find out what the sales rep's behaviour was exactly based on and then see how to communicate this back to the customers.

In summary, these examples show that ethical dilemmas need to be approached in all quadrants and at all levels. Moreover, we need to pair the (masculine) values of *discernment* (analysis of the situation) and *discipline* (obeying the rules) with the (feminine) values of *acceptance* (accepting the situation and the rules of the group) and *compassion* (care for others, for the greater groups we are part of and for the world as a whole).

CASE STUDIES

The following case studies are standard case studies taken from the Internet (see the references section at the end for the exact sources). Exactly because they are so generic makes them suitable to illustrate the use of Integral Ethics with them. I will look at the case studies walking through all four quadrants and considering them from various levels. Furthermore, I will consider the three values where needed as well.

1. DISCRIMINATION IN THE WORKPLACE

Marian, a top graduate from a famous university, was hired by a major corporation into a management position. Marian finished the corporation's management training program top in her group, and is performing above the norm in her position. She is really enjoying her work. As a black woman she feels isolated, as there are no other black women managers and few women in her area. One night at a company party she heard a conversation between two of her male co-workers and their supervisor. They were complaining to him about Marian's lack of qualifications and her unpleasant personality. They cursed affirmative action regulations for making the hiring of Marian necessary. Marian is very upset and wants to quit.

Let's look at this case in all four quadrants and see what perspectives are relevant. Starting in the lower right one, what laws are applicable here? There is mention of "affirmative action regulations," but at the same time it is doubtful if these were applied in Marian's case at all. Given that she is widely regarded as a high-performer and a very qualified manager, it can be

35

considered unlikely that affirmative action regulations (if any exist in the first place) came into play when hiring her. On the other hand, the remarks of her co-workers, no matter how unfounded they are, are not breaking any laws or regulations. Moving over to the lower left quadrant, the co-workers may be expressing something that relates to the team's or company's ethics. It would be worthwhile to find out if their remarks are exemplary of the ethical culture of the team as a whole or even of the company as a whole. A course of action for Marian to follow may be to contact her management to hear their opinion about the situation and find out whether that opinion reflects the company's ethical position. In the upper left quadrant, Marian should see if her own morality conflicts with the company's ethics. In this case, it is not clear yet if there is a conflict at all, but if there is one and it turns out that Marian's and the company's levels of ethics are in conflict with each other, it is necessary for her to consider her position and see if she wants to continue working for an organisation with ethical values that conflict with her own. Marian's behaviour (upper right quadrant) initially indicates she wants to quit, but according to this quick round through the integral model, she may want to hold off and get some more information before making up her mind. Her co-workers' behaviour is questionable from an ethical point of view, given that they seem to function at a fairly low, probably egocentric, level that excludes people that don't belong to their own small group. Given the fact that their arguments are simply not true, it is shown that their and their supervisor's behaviour is incorrect in a company that hopefully functions at least at a conventional ethical level.

It would go beyond the scope of this chapter to discuss the ethical aspects of affirmative action as such. However, it would be interesting to look at it from an integral ethical perspective that promotes the greatest depth and the greatest span, which on the one hand implies embracing the greatest number of people, such as minority groups, but at the same time should take care of not leaving other people, such as those that are part of a majority group, in the cold.

2. TAX RETURN PREPARATION

Major Certified Public Accounting (CPA) firms are known for their accuracy and competence in preparing tax returns. Each return is reviewed three times for accuracy in the tax department before it is finalized. Thus major CPA firms must charge high hourly rates, averaging $75 per hour or approximately $1,000 per return, for the preparation of returns. Clients expect the best service and advice that money can buy. During April of a specific tax year Bob, the manager of a CPA firm, assigned a young staff tax preparer, John, the responsibility of preparing a tax return for a very wealthy client who lived in Honolulu, Hawaii. In preparing a return the first step is always to look at the client's prior year's tax return to familiarize oneself with the client's sources of income and deductions. In reviewing the prior year's tax return, John noticed that the client had a $10,000 home mortgage interest expense tax deduction recorded. He telephoned the firm's client and asked very diplomatically if the client had any mortgage interest tax deduction for the current year. The client answered that he had "never had a mortgage on his home." John thanked the client and immediately walked into Bob's office and asked if an amended prior year's tax return should be prepared. Bob said, "No! Turn right on around and walk out. And remember I will deny ever having had this conversation. Have a good day!"
Let's make the rounds through the quadrants again and look at this case from all perspectives. Apparently, in the previous year, the CPA firm made a tax deduction for their client that was illegal, as it was based on a mortgage that did not exist. Given that clients' tax forms are reviewed multiple times before being

submitted to the tax authorities, multiple people must have known about this fraud and therefore the firm has broken the law. John's behaviour when he found out about what he might have thought of as an error was justified based on his findings after speaking to the client. His morality may have been at a conventional level or higher, for he clearly wanted to correct the previous year's tax return form based on the legal requirements. His manager Bob's behaviour clearly violates the law, be it because his morality is pre-conventional, viz. he is trying to cover up the firm's faults for the benefit of the firm only, or because his morality is post-conventional, viz. he disagrees with the law and thinks it is more favourable for his client, firm and society to break the law. The latter is quite unlikely, given his remark to John to keep everything silent. So we have a CPA firm here that, at least partially, functions at a pre-conventional ethical level and breaks the law where it deems it to be favourable to do so for itself and its clients.

3. POLLUTION

Joyce is the environmental compliance manager for a small plastics manufacturing company. She is currently faced with the decision whether or not to spend money on new technology that will reduce the level of a particular toxin in the wastewater that flows out the back of the factory and into a lake. The factory's emission levels are already within legal limits. However, Joyce knows that environmental regulations for this particular toxin are lagging behind scientific evidence. In fact, a scientist from the university had been quoted in the newspaper recently, saying that if emission levels stayed at this level, the fish in the lakes and rivers in the area might soon have to be declared unsafe for human consumption. Further, if companies in the region don't engage in some self-regulation on this issue, there is reason to fear that the government — backed by public opinion — may force companies to begin using the new technology, and may also begin requiring monthly emission level reports (which would be both expensive and time consuming). But the company's environmental compliance budget is tight. Asking for this new technology to be installed would put Joyce's department over-budget, and could jeopardize the company's ability to show a profit this year.

This case explores the somewhat higher levels of ethics and morality. Clearly, the company already complies with the laws when it comes to pollution of the environment. The question here is if the company is willing and able to take an extra step to preserve the environment. Joyce's point of view may be based on at least a post-conventional, if not world-centric level of morality. She clearly wants to go further than required by law (even though the law may be changed sometime soon to actually require stricter limits on emission of polluting substances). The question here is, if the company as a whole is willing to go as far as Joyce wants to go and at the same time wants to bring out the money for the new technology required for it. The real balance to be found is therefore one between a cut in the profits and the ethical position of the company towards the environment. Integral ethics requires the company to go for the greatest depth and the greatest span. This means that the environment definitely needs to be taken into account in company decisions (i.e. honouring the greatest depth). However, the interests of the company in all four quadrants also require the company to look at its own future and that of the people working in it (i.e. lower left and right quadrants, leading to an approach with the greatest span). Perhaps some creative measures need to be taken to be able to fund the environmental requirements and at the same time protect the financial interests of the company as well as the interests of the people working there. There is a balance to be found between these two aspects if the decision is to be taken based on integral ethics.

4. PERFORMANCE APPRAISALS

Frank recently became chief financial officer and a member of the Executive Committee of a medium-sized and moderately successful family-owned business. Soon after Frank started, the company decided for the first time to "right-size" to respond to rapid changes in its business. The CEO was relying on Frank to help him determine how to downsize in an ethical manner; he said he trusted Frank more on this than he did the head of his personnel department, who had "been around a little too long." On Frank's recommendation, the company decided to make its lay-off decisions based on the employees' performance scores. Each department manager would submit a list of employees ranked by the score of their last appraisals. At some point, Frank and the Executive Committee would draw a line, and those below the line would be laid off. As Frank was reviewing the evaluations, he was puzzled to find three departments in which the employee at the bottom of the list had "N/A" where the evaluation score should have been written. When he asked the managers to explain, they told him these employees had been with the company almost since the beginning. When performance appraisals had been instituted six years earlier, the CEO agreed that they keep receiving informal evaluations "as they always had." When Frank raised this issue with the CEO, he responded, "Oh, I know. I haven't really evaluated them in a long time, but it's time for them to retire anyway. They just aren't performing the way they used to. They're making pretty good money, so cutting them should let us lower the line a little and save jobs for some of the younger people"

The ethical dilemma of the company is in this case the unequal treatment of staff when it comes to performance appraisals and the use of those in redundancy planning. The dilemma of Frank is whether to make a point of that with the CEO or not. Redundancies are painful enough themselves and therefore require careful evaluation. Often, there is no clear regulation in external laws or company rules and therefore all kinds of ad hoc methods are devised by management to determine who should leave and who can stay. From my own experience, I know that even if there are applicable rules, these may lead to some valuable employees having to leave and others that are deemed less valuable staying. Therefore, it turns out that redundancy rules are often bent to accommodate the preferences of managers. In the above case, this is indeed what is happening. So in order to make downsizing ethical, it is important to establish clear (and public) methods to do so. This covers the lower right quadrant by making it clear for everyone what methods are used and why. Managers should then be held responsible for following those rules and showing the application of the rules in the results for their departments. This may lead to "favourites" having to leave and "less desired" employees staying, but in the case of a redundancy, this result needs to be taken into account when defining the rules. For instance, in one of the layoff waves that I was involved in years ago, the rule was simply "Last in, first out." This did obviously lead to the situation that people in crucial positions would have to leave. A simple rule will necessarily lead to such situations and should therefore be made more intelligent, but equally transparent, so that the company can still rely on its most valuable employees after the reductions and the employees are still clear on the rules of the layoffs. The principles of the ground, intrinsic and relative values of people, as described earlier in this chapter, come into play in this situation. It may be clear that in my opinion, the ethics surrounding redundancy planning are to be based on the conventional level of ethics in order to set clear, transparent and fair rules from the start. This is to avoid situations where individual managers, using pre-conventional morality, try to bend the rules to "save" the people from their teams that they want to keep. Obviously, care for the greatest group should include a social plan for those employees that have to leave. Not in all countries is this a requirement in the case of workforce reductions, but from a post-conventional ethical point of view, redundancy planning cannot do without taking care of the people that are leaving as best as possible. This may be done by providing assistance in finding another job, some form of financial support for a certain period, etc. Doing redundancy planning in the right and ethical way will then ensure that the greatest depth and the greatest span are honoured by keeping the process clear for the employees, keeping the company running with the people that can do so in the best way and taking care of the people that have to leave.

CONCLUSION

This chapter discussed the way in which the integral model can be applied in the field of ethics, with a specific emphasis on business ethics. Using the model and its aim to support the greatest depth and the greatest span, common business ethical dilemmas can be reviewed from all perspectives and at all required levels. It turns out that in many cases, businesses should balance their usual business interests (viz. the bottom line, or the lower right-hand side of the integral model, and the people, or the lower left side of the model) against their ethical standards. These don't always agree with each other, so the question is how far a business is willing to go honouring its ethical standards and what the effect on its business may be. Ultimately, it is hoped that striving for higher ethical standards in companies will yield more goodwill in the market and therefore increases business opportunities. The short-term business effects may however initially be negative. For individual employees, the balance to be found is that between their personal morality and the company's ethics. If these clash, an employee should consider whether this company is the right place to work for him. A balance may be found there, but if it affects the employee too much, it may be time to find a better, more ethical place to work at.

We will come back to the topic of Ethics in later chapters of this book, as its influence goes beyond what has been described in this chapter.

3. INTEGRAL PERFORMANCE MANAGEMENT

For many managers, doing the quarterly, semi-annual or yearly performance reviews with their team members is not very high on the list of favourite management tasks. This is not always to do with whether the particular manager is interested in the development of his team, for even for me as a very much people-focussed manager, the yearly performance reviews are a challenge. I believe the reason behind the reluctance of managers to do performance management is the fact that the way in which it is implemented in their companies is less than satisfactory. Performance Management in most companies seems to be at best a system based on a database interface into which standard objectives can be entered at the beginning of the year, which are subsequently forgotten for the rest of the year, until the time of the end-of-year appraisal is approaching. At times, some personal development goals ("follow this course to improve your skills") are entered along with the objectives and that's it. The painful thing that is linked to this process, however, is the fact that performance-related bonuses and salary increases are dependent on the performance management process. Then managers are rewarding their employees based on a process that is not an integral part of their daily job managing those people, is not taken serious by either manager or employee and therefore determining bonuses and salary increases becomes a highly subjective activity at the time when these rewards are to be determined.

This somewhat cynical description of the current practice of performance management shows that for many companies it is a merely administrative exercise. Nowhere in the process is it really aimed at the actual *development* of the performance of staff members.

Having undergone these processes as an employee and having utilised them as a manager, I eventually became dissatisfied with them all and started wondering if there weren't a better way of dealing with performance management that would make it less of an administrative exercise and more of a useful method that both managers and employees would be willing to use for both their benefits. This method would not only include default objectives, but also look at the employee in an integral way in the sense of the model introduced in the first chapter. After all, there is more to an employee than just his job in the narrower sense: today's work environment requires the employee to function in a variety of areas that are outside his strict job description and it requires the employer to take care of more than just making sure the job gets done. It is this that I wanted to incorporate into an integral method of performance management, which I will describe in the rest of this chapter.

METHODOLOGY

Based on the Integral Model with its four quadrants and growth in each quadrant, we would need to look at the performance of an employee in those same four quadrants. Furthermore, we need to keep in mind that development should take place in the aspects we find relevant for this employee's work activities.

The manager's first activities when doing performance management in this way is therefore first to determine what aspects he finds important in his employees' work. Traditionally, especially in the ICT industry where I come from, the focus used to be very much on knowledge, (hard) skills and "fitting into the team," but these aspects are on the one hand limited, as they cover only part of the Integral scope, and on the other hand they are vague, as they can be interpreted in many different ways.

Remember that according to the model, managers need to look at their employees from all four perspectives: their individual interior, covering aspects such as knowledge and attitude; their individual exterior, covering their physical health and behaviour; the interior of the group (the smaller scope of the team as well as the larger scope of the company or even including the customer) and finally the exterior of those groups, viz. team and company structure, politics, etc. So as a manager, you would first need to come up with relevant focus areas in these quadrants. These will likely be different depending on the actual job description, but at the same time, similar general aspects apply to employees working as an engineer and to employees working in a call-centre. It is likely the details of the general aspects that are interpreted differently for various jobs. Examples later on in this chapter will make this clearer.

Once the manager has defined these focus areas of the employees' jobs, picking them from across the four quadrants of the Integral Model, it is time to assess their current level. Note that whatever aspect we choose to assess an employee on, it is possible to develop oneself in that aspect and therefore, some measure of the current level should be possible to define. I propose a general set of five levels, numbered from 0 (indicating the starting level) to 5 (indicating expert level for that job), to indicate the level of experience, knowledge or other development in these aspects. It would be most constructive to have this assessment done not only by the manager, but also by the employee himself and in a meeting get agreement on the current level. In my experience, it turned out that I generally assessed my team members to be at a higher level than they assessed themselves and this led to interesting discussions.

Having agreed on a starting level for all aspects that are relevant to the job, the next step is to agree where you and the employee want him to be at the end of the appraisal period. This period is typically a year, with one or more intermediate review sessions in between, so setting SMART (the well-known acronym meaning Specific, Measurable, Attainable, Realistic and Time-bound) objectives is the thing to do here. Note, however, that for many aspects, it is very difficult, if not impossible, to define real SMART objectives, as some parts of the employees' development are less tangible than others. This situation already indicates a difference between what is referred to as "Objectives," which are goals that can generally be described in SMART terms, and "Expectations and Requirements," which are the less tangible aspects of the job that are harder to catch in SMART development goals. Later in this chapter I will present a method to capture expectations and requirements in a format similar to SMART, but more suited to the less tangible goals. In any case, the current and target levels of all aspects should be described as specifically as possible in a joint effort of manager and employee.

This should conclude the setting of objectives, expectations and requirements in the integral performance management method. Note that the main difference with classic performance management is the scope of this method. Integral performance management requires the manager and the employee to look at all aspects that are relevant to the job and set development goals for those. How that is different in practice will follow from the next section that goes into more detail about what all those other aspects are exactly.

EMPLOYEE DEVELOPMENT IN THE FOUR QUADRANTS

This section will deal with defining several aspects in all quadrants of the Integral Model that are relevant for an employee's performance on the job. You will see that some of them are familiar and others are often disregarded in classic performance management. Also, some of them are relevant to all sorts of jobs and others are more specific to a particular job role. I will provide examples of the integral development for various roles to illustrate this. Note that an infinite number of focus areas can be defined, depending on the actual job and on the individual performing the job and his needs.

In general, the following aspects can be defined in the four quadrants as relevant for any employee.

Internal Individual:	External Individual :
• Attitude • Knowledge • Ethics	• Health • Behaviour
Internal Collective:	External Collective:
• Communication • Cooperation • Culture	• Organisation • Politics

Examples of development lines in each quadrant of the Integral Model.

In the figure above, I have defined nine generic aspects of any employee's functioning in any organisation. To clarify what is meant with these items, below follows a fuller description of each one of them. This is necessary in order to make these aspects as clear as possible and hence be able to assess employees and create development plans for them.

Attitude. Attitude refers to the general approach to the job, the colleagues and the customer. It is made visible by observing various aspects that are partially present in other quadrants, such as communication and behaviour, but also has less tangible aspects in it that are not clearly present in other quadrants, such as flexibility, setting priorities, time management and setting boundaries. A full discussion of attitude is part of the chapter on Leadership later in this book. Many of these aspects are hard to measure objectively and therefore an assessment of the current level and if needed a development plan in this line need to be agreed between manager and employee based on concrete examples. Development in this area is quite difficult to make objective as well, apart from training in using certain tools as part of e.g. time management and prioritising. Development of attitude is therefore often made explicit in terms of its resulting *behaviour*, which is part of the upper right quadrant.

Knowledge. This is often the easiest aspect to assess, given that most jobs require a certain level of knowledge. Often, knowledge can be expressed in terms of obtaining certain industry certificates (such as CCNA, ITIL, PMI, etc.). However, knowledge alone does not necessarily say anything about performance on the job. Some candidates who I did job interviews with showed all kinds of certifications on their CV, while having a total lack of practical, hands-on experience with the technologies covered by those certifications. So again in this aspect, the (static) knowledge cannot be seen apart from the practical job performance, which is covered by the *behaviour* aspect in the upper right quadrant. Development of knowledge can be stimulated in the form of (external or internal) classroom trainings, knowledge exchange within a team, permitting study leave, sponsoring books, etc.

Ethics. As described in the previous chapter, ethics is in my opinion the most widely misunderstood aspect of today's business environment. However, it is also the aspect that has received a lot of focus in the past ten years or so, due to the occurrence of unethical practices in many companies. As explained before, at its most basic level, ethics is about *compliance* with external laws and regulations. At the best level, ethics is understood in terms of the company's ethical standards, the possible contrast thereof with the individual employee's moral standards, the employees' behaviour in an ethical sense and the ethical level of external laws and regulations. Note that most if not all decisions we take have some ethical aspect to them that has an impact on how we choose to deal with a given situation we find ourselves in. And therefore our decisions depend on the ethical level we function at. Apart from creating a baseline in the form of a code of conduct, development in ethics can best be done by creating awareness of what it really involves, rather than organising a series of training courses that are merely aimed at compliance. The chapter on ethics in this book tries to create this awareness and could therefore be used as a starting point for work in this area.

Health. Health management is generally implemented in the form of counting sick days and having a company doctor visiting at times to assess chronic cases. This is somewhat limited. The health of an employee affects his performance on the job and an increased number of sick days is often more a reflection of dissatisfaction with the job than of real physical problems. In that way, health and attitude are linked to each other. Physical health can be promoted in various ways. In the first place, a company needs to implement *active* sickness leave policies, meaning that health of the employees is monitored more closely and deviations from the standard are flagged at an earlier stage. Given the relationship between health and attitude, a solution for health problems that are not strictly physical but e.g. also have a motivational aspect is to simply have a discussion about it and jointly define ways to improve the situation. Other things to promote physical health are providing an in-house gym or sponsor the membership of sports clubs. At the same time, nutrition is the basis of a healthy lifestyle, so having a company restaurant with healthy food is something very basic that a company can do to keep its staff healthy.

Behaviour. Behaviour is the reflection of many other development lines and is the most apparent of abilities that an employee can show. What constitutes "good" or "bad" behaviour is a matter of definition.

A baseline for it can in a way be found in the Codes of Conduct that many companies have written nowadays. These Codes are lightly embedded in a sense of company ethics, as described before, but are generally not enough to determine the employees' behaviour at all times. Behaviour has to do with attitude, ethics, communication, cooperation, politics, etc. and as such cannot be seen in isolation. Examples of behaviour should be used to assess those other aspects, though, so that it can be determined and agreed what kind of behaviour is desirable and what kind of behaviour is to be avoided. In order to improve behaviour, it should then be assessed what the deeper motivation or background of the non-desirable behaviour was and that background can then be linked to one of the other lines of development, such as ethics, attitude, politics, etc.

Communication. One of the first things I learnt in my career, where I was always working at large companies, was that a lack of communication is at the root of most trouble at the workplace. It also soon became clear to me that there is more to communication than talking to each other: communication is about the useful exchange of relevant information. In today's office environment, there are numerous ways in which people can communicate and equally many ways to use those tools in the wrong way. A quick look around my desk and on my computer reveals a landline phone, a mobile phone, two e-mail clients, an instant messenger, shared network drives, numerous SharePoints, an infinite number of internal and external websites, netconferencing and conference calling facilities and, last but not least, actual real life conversations either at the coffee machine or in other settings. The first key to proper communication is: knowing when to use any of these facilities and with whom. The second key to proper communication is: knowing *how* to communicate. The latter is more subtle than the former, for it deals with such things as learning to see things from the other person's perspective while not losing your own, avoiding unnecessary conflicts while making your point clear, keeping the communication at a professional level, etc. There are plenty of training sessions out there that are based on principles like Neuro-Linguistic Programming, Transactional Analysis or other methods that can at least create awareness of one's communication patterns and are then supposed to lead to actual improvements in those patterns so that one becomes a more proficient communicator. Refer to the chapter about Coaching and Communication for more about this subject.

Cooperation. Some people work best when they are left alone and not bothered by others. If you are writing a book, like I am doing right now, this is understandable and fine. However, in the average office environment, daily life is full of colleagues, managers, project leaders and various others who need to work with you. Many projects are done with multiple people involved that need to exchange information, depend on each other's output, need to get aligned, or in short: who need to cooperate. Cooperation is therefore a basic ability of any employee and as such needs to be part of an integral performance assessment. Attitude is again the aspect that forms the foundation of the ability to cooperate, but more practically, cooperation also consists of working in or as a team, being responsive to requests and sharing knowledge and experience with the own team, other teams or with the customer. These are very practical activities based on which it can be seen how someone performs at the aspect of cooperation.

Culture. Every person has a background in a certain culture. Every society has a certain culture. Every company has a culture, too, and so does every team and every single member of the team. By default, therefore, everyone works in a multicultural environment. Just like in general society, multicultural environments can provide enrichment or cause friction. Enrichment is found when the best out of all cultural environments is combined to form an even better organisation.

Friction is caused when cultures clash, when a dominant culture, such as that of the company, conflicts with values from a different culture, such as that of the employee. For employees, it is often a matter of "surviving" in a company's culture, given that it is easier to adapt as an individual than to change the culture of the greater organisation. As a manager, you have more influence on the culture in the team to solve these conflicts, but individual employees may have a hard time adapting to a given culture. Part of the ability of coping with culture is also working with people from various cultural backgrounds, in which case the cultural differences may appear very close and direct. At the same time, having managed a team of up to 170 people with 20 to 30 different cultural backgrounds, I know that such an organisation can be a wonderful environment that provides an opportunity to look at things from very many different perspectives and as such stimulates productivity. Finally, culture needs to be kept in mind when working in international settings across multiple time zones. Approaching a German customer is something wholly different from approaching a French one, for instance. Again, attitude is an important basis for the proper approach of the cultural line of development.

Organisation. Knowing the organisation in which you work is important in order to be able to find your way in it, get the right contacts and be able to cooperate in an effective way. Typically, in an organisation producing something (be it a physical product or a service), there are various teams doing part of the production in a certain sequence. The first thing to know is obviously the own organisation, but soon after that, it becomes relevant to get to know the organisations that are immediately before or immediately after the own organisation in the production flow. This increases understanding of their relevance and makes it clearer where the interfaces between the own organisation and the other organisations are. More importantly, it provides for clarity about the exact responsibilities of each group, so that it prevents activities falling in between the cracks of groups' responsibilities (or being done twice, for that matter). Another aspect of organisation is how to deal with the company's structure. If there is a big hierarchy in the company you work for, you need to know how to deal with it. For example, it can be very frustrating having to wait for approvals from a manager seven layer above your head, but if that is required as per company policy you will have to deal with it. It is of course useful to point out possible issues with this approach, but the decision to change it is above your head. Finally, when you work intensively with customers, it will become necessary to get to know the customers' organisation as well as possible, too. Similar to the own organisation, this clarifies responsibilities and provides the right interfaces for you to work with.

Politics. Politics are the joy of every organisation, no matter what size. For some odd reason everybody complains about politics in the office, but at the same time everybody takes part in it in some way. The issue is that every person has his personal interests, is part of a group with certain (overlapping, but also often different) interests, and is also part of the wider company that has again additional interests. These interests are not always aligned, although ideally, they should be part of each other: the company's interests should include the team's interests, which should in turn include the personal interests. Life isn't that easy, though, so in practice, there are a whole lot of hidden or double agendas out there – not necessarily in a purely negative sense, but certainly in a way that it influences decision making of most people. Being aware of this *in yourself* is one step in dealing with it. Being aware of it in others is the next step. From this awareness comes the ability to deal with it and reduce it as much as possible. Obviously, politics becomes more apparent at higher levels in the organisation, but lower levels will be confronted with it in a sense as well.

For specific roles in an organisation, other development lines can be defined that are more appropriate for the roles in question. The following is an example of additional items for a Manager responsible for both people management and business management:

Internal Individual:	External Individual :
• Leadership • Empathy • Analytical Skills	• Example behaviour • Escalation handling
Internal Collective:	**External Collective:**
• Fostering team culture • People Management	• Team organisation • Setting procedures and standards • Account Management

Examples of additional development lines in each quadrant for a Manager.

A different example of additional skills is the one for a Customer Services Representative:

Internal Individual:	External Individual:
• Politeness • Analysis of customer issues	• Telephone handling and behaviour

Internal Collective:	External Collective:
• Ability to see issue from the customer's perspective • Customer communication	• Knowing the call-handling and ticketing procedures • Effective escalation management

Examples of development lines in each quadrant for a Customer Services Representative.

These additional development lines are quite self-explanatory, so I will not go into details of them here.

Something that became clear from the previous examples is that you need to realise that the development lines are not completely independent of each other. In fact, the skills in the Internal Individual quadrant are often the basis needed to develop skills in the other quadrants. Without empathy, fostering a team culture is hard to do. Without analytical skills, organising the team and setting procedures and standards for it are difficult to achieve. Similarly, Attitude and Behaviour are often the result of Ethics, Communication and Cooperation, to name a few.

Depending on the level of an employee, all these aspects could be expected to be developed up to a certain point: for more senior employees this point is at a further developed level than for more junior ones. It is therefore important to specify for each job role what the minimum and maximum level of development in all these aspects is considered to be. Practically spoken, this means that a level 5 in communication means something different for an operational engineer than for a senior manager - the expectations at level 5 are lower for the former than for the latter. Once we have specified these, the "Expectations and Requirements" part of performance management is covered.

PUTTING IT INTO PRACTICE: TOOLS

As mentioned at the beginning of this chapter, performance management deals with objectives and with expectations and requirements. Tracking and measuring these aspects requires some practical tools. Objectives as defined in most classic performance management tools are to be worded in a way that these are made measurable. However, some of the other aspects as defined above are much harder to measure objectively. I would therefore propose to not try the impossible and make immeasurable items measurable, but to focus on agreement between employee and manager on items that require growth and how that growth is to be achieved throughout the year. The general methodology for it has been described above already, but the practical side of it can be implemented as follows.

Make a list of aspects that are relevant in the job of an employee. Show these aspects as lines of development in the relevant quadrant of the Integral Model. The picture below is one that I made in a simple drawing tool that shows the four quadrants, five levels of development (the concentric circles) and arrows extending to the current level for each relevant line of development.

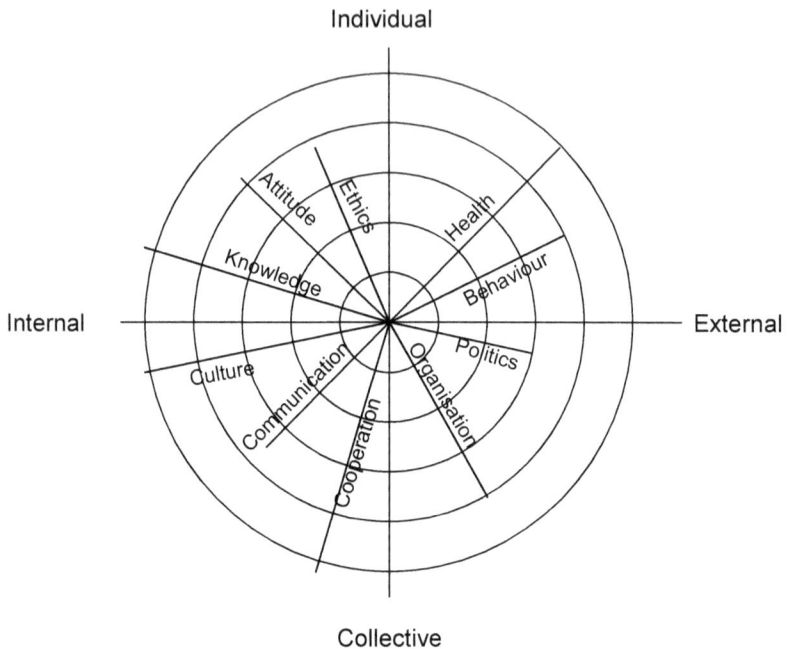

An Integral Performance Graph.

Note that the "score" of an employee is to be determined jointly by the employee himself and the manager, so that an agreement is reached on where the employee is in his development at this moment. Based on this picture, areas for improvement can be identified. For instance, in the picture above Politics and Communication are relatively poorly developed. Targets for this improvement should be given in a similar way as the current state was assessed, resulting and a delta between the current state and the desired state. In MS-Excel, the Integral Performance Graph can be plotted in the form of a (double) spider web diagram, which looks as follows.

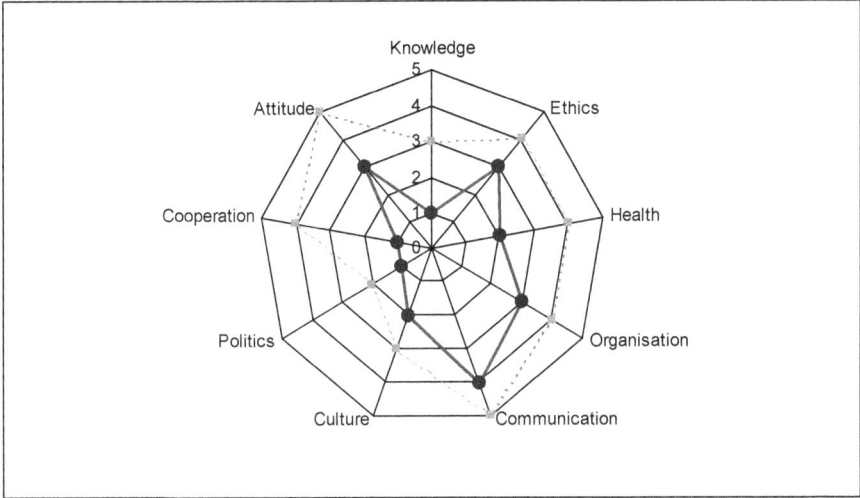

An Integral Performance Graph as a spider web diagram.

This spider web diagram is easily constructed in MS-Excel. Unfortunately, it doesn't show the lines of development in their respective quadrant, but it is easy to see from the inner graph, which shows the current development, and the outer graph, which shows target development, where growth is needed.

To determine the employee's development opportunities, an *Integral Development Plan* (IDP) is written, in which activities for further development of each aspect can be described. The following table is an IDP on which the above spider web diagram was based. You see the aspects of development that were assessed in the first column. The second column lists the current level that was assessed by the employee and his manager. The target development levels are listed in the third column. The last column contains a brief description of how to get from the current level to the target level. This brief description should be expanded in a more extensive and detailed development plan.

Skill	Current	Target	Planned Activities
Knowledge	1	3	Study for CCNP
Ethics	3	4	Study what Ethics involves and act on it
Health	2	4	Go to the gym, eat healthy food at the canteen
Behaviour	3	5	Become more pro-active in projects.
Organisation	3	4	Get to know the org chart, organise meetings with departments we work with
Communication	4	5	Get to know NLP techniques to improve communication
Culture	2	3	Find ways to deal with other people's cultures in the office
Politics	1	2	Learn to understand why some people say one thing and do another thing
Cooperation	1	4	Learn to share work and knowledge, do projects together with others
Attitude	3	5	Get new inspiration for the daily job requirements

An Integral Development Plan (IDP).

Part of the IDP should also be timelines for the realisation of growth. Depending on the specific aspect, growth may require more time than the evaluation period permits. So the ultimate level (number 5) for this job role need not be indicated in the "Target" column if growth extends to a couple of years, for instance.

Given the nature of the development aspects assessed, it may be difficult to describe the development plan in a detailed way. A method to overcome this is the Outcome Frame, which is the default goal-setting methodology used in NLP.

Helping to Achieve Goals – The Outcome Frame

The Outcome Frame (which is yet another ugly NLP-expression that can best be translated as "framework for attaining goals") is the ideal tool for coaching and is even as popular as being practically the only thing some coaching books talk about. Also in the context of counselling, it is important to be able to formulate development goals correctly to be able to realise them. In fact, the outcome frame is nothing more than a very specific type of objective that is somewhat similar to the, in commercial companies well-known, SMART Objectives ("SMART" being an acronym for Specific, Measurable, Attainable, Realistic, Time-bound).

However, in NLP, this is formulated somewhat differently, based on five criteria that guide the creation of an outcome. The aim is to define the target situation (the "outcome state") starting from the current situation (the "problem state") and define all the steps in between to get from the problem state to the outcome state. These five criteria are as follows:

1. *The outcome needs to be put in positive terms.* So, it needs to be written in terms of what needs to be achieved, not in terms of what you want to get rid of. This is to do with the fact that the human brains don't seem to be able to interpret words such as "no" and "not" and therefore, when a sentence is being processed in which

---

those words are present, the opposite is achieved: "do not" becomes "do." For example, the following sentence is not permitted in an outcome: "I do not want to do this boring work anymore," but it should be translated into something stated positively, such as: "I want to find work in which I can function independently."

2. *The outcome needs to be within the own realm of influence.* It is nice to sit down and write an outcome in which you say that other people are going to realise it for you and you don't need to do anything yourself, but in practice, this has no purpose. When you formulate the outcome, it needs to be clear that you are going to act on it yourself. So and outcome that states "I don't want to be bullied anymore" should be changed into "I want to be able to defend myself against people bullying me." Apart from this, you can discuss the definition of the own realm of influence – how much influence do we in fact have on the world around us? These discussions do, however, often lead to large numbers of spiritual assumptions that are more to do with individual beliefs than with objective reality. For a discussion at that level, I refer the reader to the chapter about Transpersonal Therapy. For the purpose of the discussion of the outcome frame, it just needs to be understood that we need to act ourselves on whatever we write in our outcomes if we want it to become reality.

3. *There needs to be a measurable, tangible result of the outcome.* So you need to be able to perceive with our senses that the outcome has become successful. What is it that you hear, see, feel and notice otherwise at the moment that our goal has been achieved? When exactly is the outcome complete? Are any other people involved in it? In what context and in what environment do you want to achieve our outcome? This is a step towards making the outcome more specific, so that there cannot be any doubt about what needs to be done exactly to get where we want to be.

4. *What is the first concrete step to be taken to realise the outcome?* From this step onwards, all other necessary steps can be defined as well. The aim is to define the path from the current state to the

outcome state. Note that this step often leads to additional outcomes to specify the steps in between more fully.

5. Finally, *Ecology*. A bit further in this chapter I will describe in more detail what ecology means in the context of Integral Therapy, but for the outcome, it is sufficient to define it as the need to check whether the outcome has a negative impact on yourself, other people or the environment. What is the motivation of your wanting to realise the outcome? Are you and other served with it or is there any harm done in realising it? What is the *outcome sequitor*, the value that satisfied when realising the outcome?

Using the steps I just described, you can define an outcome on several levels. It can be something that is quite specific from the start, such as writing a book (and yes, I did write an outcome before starting to write this book – see below) or it can be something quite vague to start with, like wanting to be able to deal with an illness. The five items above can then be used more or less concretely to help define the outcome. At the moment that the outcome has been concretely defined and conforms to all five criteria, it practically does not need to be looked at anymore. Inside ourselves, we have prepared ourselves sufficiently to achieve the outcome and it will turn out that it will actually happen. That is nothing to do with magic, but more with mental conditioning to achieve what we want to achieve.

A small example of an outcome, specifically the one I made for writing this book, is the following.

Outcome: writing the book "Integral Management"
Summary: to have written a book in one year's time about Integral Management that is ready to be published.
Own realm of influence: This outcome is fully within my own realm of influence, because I am writing the book myself. Proof-reading by

others is outside my direct influence, but needs to be initiated by myself and is strictly spoken an optional part of writing the book.

Steps to achieve the outcome:

1. Create an outline;
2. Collect sources;
3. Expand to a readable text;
4. Make side-bars (case-studies, expansions, excursions, etc.);
5. Find proof-readers and gather feedback from them;
6. Incorporate feedback into the book;
7. Prepare the book for sending it off to publishers or self-publish.

Measurable result: All steps 1-4 and 6-7 can be verified by writing it all on paper. Step 5 can be verified by convincing colleagues and laymen to read the manuscript and send me feedback.

Ecology: writing the book is positive for me, because it shapes my ideas and simulates my development and creativity. It can be positive for others in terms of enriching my professional group, colleagues and other interested people. It has no negative impact on me, others or the environment as far as I know.

OTHER APPLICATIONS

After developing the IDP system, it turned out I could use the principles of it in a number of other areas as well. I will list them here briefly to give you an idea of how to take these ideas a few steps further.

JOB DESCRIPTIONS

Given the relevance of the elements of the IDP I described, it is surprising how most job descriptions, CVs and job interviews only seem to focus on knowledge and hardly on aspects such as attitude, communication, politics, etc. Knowing what these aspects involve in the office, it is possible to write a job description incorporating these items and performing interviews with candidates based on those aspects. So my job descriptions today are pretty lengthy, asking for experience and skills in all areas that I have defined in people's IDPs as well.

RECRUITMENT AND PROMOTIONS

These job descriptions of course feedback immediately into the recruitment process. I have worked with one of our recruiters on creating job profiles for the various functions in my organisation. Just as is the case with CVs, these profiles originally focussed on mostly knowledge and a few vague aspects of leadership (see a later chapter for more about what leadership really involves). These job profiles now range from the most junior positions up to Director's level, incorporating all the categories defined in the IDPs for Engineers and their management. This creates a comprehensive job family, with which it is possible to determine exactly what level a job applicant requires to be eligible for a vacancy. But also, it serves as guidance for existing employees who may be ready for a promotion, if the opportunity is there.

360-DEGREES FEEDBACK

After introducing the IDP, I developed feedback forms that everyone in my organisation was required to send out to people they had worked with outside their own team. These feedback forms were set up along the same categories as the items in the IDP, with the request to the person filling them out to score the employee on a scale of 1 to 5 on each of the categories and leaving specific feedback about what their experiences were as well. This linked exactly into the mid-year and year-end reviews, providing the managers with insight into how other people in- and outside the company had perceived working with our employees.

TALENT MANAGEMENT

Talent Management is a broader area, which I will extensively deal with in the next chapter. It will not be surprising that both the Integral Model and the IDP system serve as an important basis for setting up a proper talent management programme.

EXIT INTERVIEWS

The other end of the spectrum is the aspect of firing people: knowing the aspects that are required to do the job properly makes it possible to more quickly identify areas where growth is needed. If growth is lacking despite it having been identified in the IDP, it may be necessary to terminate employment. The message to the employee that is to be laid off can then be based on very clear aspects that have been agreed before so should not come as a surprise anymore.

4. TALENT MANAGEMENT

INTRODUCTION

Talent Management within many companies is currently seen as a yearly administrative exercise where people are identified as "High Potential", "Emerging Talent" or some other similar expression, but it is as such an exercise with no immediate consequences on either the individual or the manager or the company. Apart from the odd training specifically dedicated to High Potential employees, no further actions are planned as a result of this talent marking exercise.

Moreover, Talent Management is an isolated activity that is not linked to overall Performance Management, Personal Development or Compensation Planning.

I perceive a need for improvement here, specifically aimed at High Potential employees, but also applicable to all other employees. Companies are putting more and more pressure onto their staff and often do very little in return, especially for those that are willing to go out of their way to achieve the company's goals and have it in them to go far in the organisation.

This chapter was originally set up as a discussion paper for use inside my company and makes suggestions on how to take Talent Management a step further, for the benefit of both the employees involved and the company. I had done interviews with both highly talented employees and with Human Resource (HR) managers from a number of large companies for this purpose, for whose cooperation I am very grateful. It has now turned into a chapter of this book, hopefully being useful for other companies as well.

A remark to start with: talent management is presented here in the context of people having talent to grow towards leadership positions. People may have all sorts of other talents besides leadership potential, such as technical capabilities, but these are typically not assessed as part of talent management. Therefore, this chapter focusses on talent for leadership positions only.

In the excellent book "High Flyers," Morgan McCall summarises the general approach to Talent Management in a single sentence. He writes, "…people with the *ability* to learn from *experience*, when given key experiences as determined by the *business strategy*, will learn the *needed skills* if given the right kind of *support*" (all indicated emphasis is mine). This summarises the need to have a talent management framework that provides the right people with the experiences they need to develop their skills and knowledge, which is embedded in the overall business strategy and has a support structure in place to bring the talented people where these employees and the company want them to be.

It is around these elements that I will propose a framework of talent management in this chapter.

A framework for effective Talent Management should take into account what role is envisaged for Talent Management within the overall business outcomes of the company. After all, the business outcomes are leading for whatever is done in the company and therefore Talent Management cannot be seen in isolation thereof.

In my experience, this connection has not always been established, so we should start by defining what role Talent Management has within the overall business outcomes of the company.

For lack of commonly established principles about the role of Talent Management within many companies' business outcomes, I will make the following assumptions in the remainder of this chapter:

1. Talent Management is to be used to grow a pool of potential future leaders for the company;

2. Future leaders are to be sourced partially from the company itself and partially from outside the company. An exact mix is to be determined, but irrelevant in the present context;
3. Future leaders should have a broad background in the company as well as broad skills, meaning that they should not only have in-depth knowledge of a single area, but (also) of many other relevant areas in the company.

These principles are at the basis of a talent management framework that should develop the capabilities of leaders in all quadrants onto the desired levels. A proposed framework taking all this into account will be presented next.

The principles, framework and talent management in general don't exist in isolation nor are they the responsibility of a single person or department. They need to be carried by three main groups in the company though: the individual employees, their management and "the company," in this case often represented by Human Resources. Their individual roles are described in what follows as well.

THE INTEGRAL TALENT MANAGEMENT FRAMEWORK

This section provides a framework of talent management along the lines of the Integral Model. It therefore looks at all relevant aspects of talent management from the perspectives of internal development, external behaviour, the company's culture and the company's structure. The elements of this framework look as follows.

Define what role talent management has within the overall business outcomes of the company
First of all, the position of talent management in the company needs to be established. Just like everything else, this should be seen as part of the overall business outcomes of the company. A number of

guiding principles for the role of talent management can be the following, leading to a talent management policy:

1. High Potential Talent should be developed within the company with the objective of filling the higher leadership positions with experienced people rather than bringing in externals. This limited number of employees should therefore get absolute priority to assume leadership positions once they become available and should be actively assisted in developing themselves to the desired levels expected from leaders.

2. At the same time, a healthy balance between internally developed leaders and external ones should be established in a ratio of e.g. 80% vs. 20% respectively. This is because bringing in external leadership is indispensable to introduce fresh perspectives to the organisation.

3. High Potential Talent helps the company achieve its business outcomes by consistently showing a focus on the main drivers of the business.

4. Talent Management should be linked to the company's business strategy by clearly defining what is expected from leaders within the context of that strategy. Taking it a step further, existing leadership may be assessed for their strengths and weaknesses and gaps identified that need to be filled with new talented people.

Define the exact criteria of highly talented people in concrete terms
Existing talent management systems often use concise definitions of what talent means to a company. This results in individual managers trying to identify talent using their own interpretation of talent, which in turn means that there is no consistent approach to identifying talent. Some issues with a lack of definition of talent are as follows:

1. There is no timeline defined for growth to the target level: is someone a talented if he can move 2 hierarchical levels up in twenty years from now or is the qualification based on a 5-year window?

2. There is no indication of what skills are required for positions two levels up – often these are Director and VP positions, for which job descriptions and requirements are rarely published. It is then hard to assess if an employee has potential to develop those skills in a certain timeframe or not.

3. Paired to the previous item, what exactly is the envisaged profile of a talented employee? A generic definition is far too vague and therefore open to interpretation in various ways. There is a need to clarify this so people from one organisation get assessed according to the same type of criteria as people from another organisation.

4. Based on the lack of information about timeline, profile and requirements, it is also not clear what percentage of the population would typically be identified as highly talented. This has implications for the size of a programme for these employees and also for their future perspective in the organisation: given that the aim is for highly talented employees to grow towards higher management positions, what is the number of people required to eventually fill open positions at those levels?

These issues imply we have to go beyond the usual one-sentence definition and indicate very clearly what is expected from a leader at Director or VP level.

A generic job description of a Director and a VP should be made available along the lines of the Integral Development Plan discussed in the previous chapter. Moreover, there should be clear behavioural indicators that can be turned into a development path for highly talented people. Examples of such indicators may be:

- Expresses oneself in a clear and concise manner, both at the level of executive management and at the operational level;
- Can work under extreme pressure, both in terms of time and in terms of balancing many priorities;
- Acts as an advocate for the company within the industry by participating as a speaker in trade shows, technology forums, etc.

- Has knowledge of the business at MBA level and bases decisions on information from various areas including technology, finance, economics, legal aspects, HR, etc.

Based on statements like these, it should be clear what kind of capabilities are expected from executive leaders and a gap analysis can be made by the employee that can in turn lead to a concrete development plan in these areas.

Define what percentage of the organisation on average is expected to be Highly Talented
A general target of the total population who are to be considered "highly talented" seems to be 10%, but this depends on the hierarchy of the organisation. Flatter organisations need fewer people at the top, so the bar of what constitutes talent that can grow towards higher leadership positions can be set higher than for very hierarchical organisations that need a lot of higher management. This percentage is arbitrary, though. Your company may be in the situation where you have a lot of talent available, but are unable to accommodate them for leadership functions. Or otherwise, there may be too little talent available to fill the available leadership positions. In both cases, sticking to a strict percentage is nonsense. Similar to performance management, talent should be assessed in an objective way, based on objective measures; it should not be forged to fit a statistical distribution.

Set a timeline for the development of talent towards a leadership position
A missing element in many talent management systems is when exactly people earmarked as "highly talented" are supposed to be at the required level. If the criterion is for highly talented employees to be able to grow towards a Director or Vice President level, then in what period of time is this expected? Employees who can grow

towards that position from the same starting point in one year can likely be considered more talented than employees who need five years to do so. So the definition of "highly talented" should include a measure of how much time it may take a person to grow to a certain stage of leadership.

Identify talent at an early stage
Many companies have their periodic Talent Management cycle, which takes place one a year or once every other year. This exercise requires managers to indicate the talent levels of their employees. Often companies have a certain number of levels defined indicating the potential of their employees to grow towards leadership positions. Whatever the definition of these levels, it is up to the manager to identify talent throughout the year, not only at a set moment. Moreover, talent should be identified as soon as possible, meaning that already during job interviews, highly talented people should be identified in order to help them immediately with their further development.

Indicate the need to discuss talent ratings with the involved employees and link that discussion to what this means for the employee.
In my opinion, talent ratings should be discussed with the employee. This may sound straightforward, but I have noticed it is not common practice. The rating should not just be presented as an earmark, but rather as a means to get into a dialogue with the employee about his career path and the possibilities to develop him towards a certain leadership position.
In the last part of the previous sentence there is an obvious catch, as the question is what possibilities there are exactly, both in terms of career possibilities and in terms of a framework to support highly skilled employees in their development. Therefore, the framework

should first be in place, so that the manager can inform the employee properly about the meaning of being marked as a "high potential."

Employees to determine their own Needs
The first action for a new employee to take is, whether he is considered highly talented or not, to determine what his expectations of his job and career are. This can also be expressed as a determination of his needs. "Needs" from a developmental perspective leads us easily to the work Abraham Maslow did, creating a general hierarchy of needs. This hierarchy is well-known and can also be adapted to talent as follows.

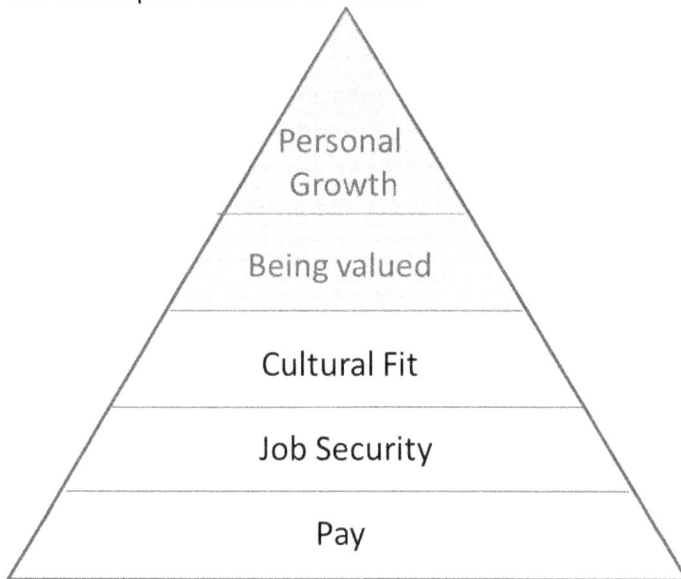

Maslow's Hierarchy of Needs adapted to talent.

The base of the pyramid is composed of the things that are most basic to our needs: first of all the salary, quickly followed by job security. A bit higher up in the hierarchy is the right fit in the team and the company. Once these three levels have been satisfied, employees typically focus on their value in the company, how they value the company and are valued by others. Beyond this, the top of the hierarchy is formed by the personal growth of the employee.

It turns out that highly talented people don't worry about the lower levels in the hierarchy, but most likely primarily focus on the upper two levels. This is exemplified by a short survey I have done among some of my employees that were marked as highly talented people. The feedback from the team about what they needed from a talent management programme was as follows:

• *Goals*, so the individual can trace the path by evaluating and determining the areas that need to be improved.
• Motivation related to *personal and job growth.*
• Investment in terms of funding of *education*, management support for *personal development.*
• Have a mind-set to be more engaged to *look forward and grow* within the role.
• *Challenges* where leadership skills are required.
• *Opportunities* to perform in a leadership role.
• Meet other talented employees to *share experiences* on how we are developing ourselves, and meeting the challenges of a leadership role.
• Formal leadership *training*, focussed on highly talented employees.
• *Mentoring* by a leader.

In fact, one of the items goes beyond even this model and indicates that there is a need for *collective* growth rather than just individual growth. This shows that leadership is not an individual characteristic, but should really be seen as a collective effort.

Another way of looking at things is the following figure from Oscar Berg. It shows an interesting contrast between the often perceived needs of highly skilled employees and their real needs. It turns out that the real needs are very much aligned with the top of Maslow's pyramid.

WHAT MAKES KNOWLEDGE WORKERS PRODUCTIVE?

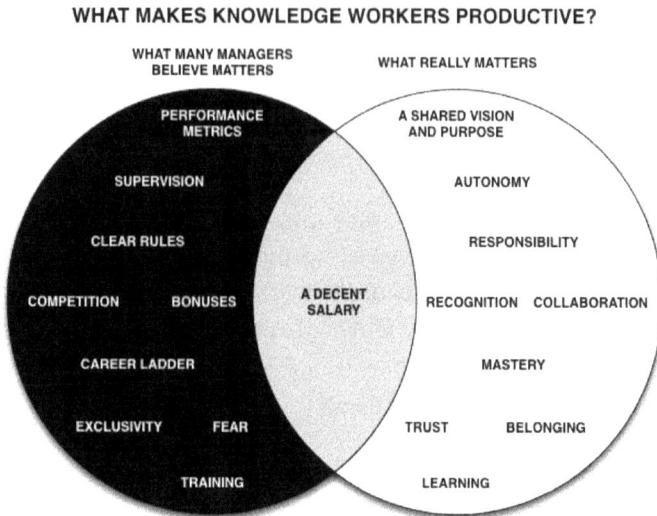

What makes knowledge workers productive?

Whatever the needs are, the employee should be aware of them and be able to act on them by determining ways to fulfil those needs. This leads to the creation of a development plan.

Create an Integral Development Plan
Creating a proper development plan is in line with the Integral Development Plan (IDP), discussed previously in the chapter on Integral Performance Management. The IDP provides a wider view of the capabilities of people, and should cover all the essential qualities that are required in leaders. Given that this section is listed under the employee's responsibilities, it is indeed my opinion that the creation

of a development plan is primarily the employee's responsibility. After all, it is the employee who knows best what his needs are and therefore it is him who can best indicate the ways to develop areas where growth is needed. It is up to the manager to determine possible gaps that the employee did not see and support him in his development.

Set career targets
As an employee, you need to think about what you want to do with your life and with your career. Note that this is not a one-time exercise: targets can change all the time. In my own case, for instance, I have had the target to grow towards higher management functions and was on my way to get there. Then it turned out that in my company, going another level up would involve me in activities that were very demotivating for me, so I took a step back and am now in a position that is more consultative in nature. I feel much happier now and have also changed my career targets away from growing into higher management to becoming a proper consultant to higher management. Career targets are therefore dynamic and need to be revised regularly.

Coach the employee
The main role for the manager after identifying talent in his team is to coach the highly talented ones among them in a more intensive way. Coaching should be a regular activity for a manager, but is more important for highly skilled employees (as well as for low-skilled ones).
Note that Coaching and Mentoring are different in this respect: in my definition, coaching aims at bringing out the required internal resources and qualities from a person without giving direction. Mentoring is more about showing how things are to be done, giving guidance and actively helping to resolve issues. Mentoring should be done by a person outside the team, not by the direct manager, and

can therefore include discussions about the relationship between the employee and the manager. Coaching is the primary task of the direct manager.

Coaching a highly talented employee involves regular checkpoints (e.g. bi-weekly) to discuss issues the employee ran into, focus on personal development and career progression and stimulate the employee to find his own way inside the company and find opportunities for growth himself.

Coach the manager
Coaching does not come natural for most managers. Management development should therefore also focus on this aspect of being a manager. In the next chapter I will go deeply into what being a coaching manager means in general. Coaching talent requires an even greater focus on coaching techniques, though. Therefore, the manager should be well-prepared for his coaching tasks and this is a task for the company to provide training on.

Establish career paths for all job functions, both for highly talented and for regular employees
Do all employees know what their career perspective is exactly? Is there awareness of the possibility to grow not only hierarchically (upwards) but also at the same level (laterally)? Whatever the function, if people are eager to grow further (a first sign of them being suitable for a more demanding job), they should know where they can grow to, what is required to get there and what possibilities exist to actually move to a new position. To enable this, career paths should be established, showing for each function what the possibilities are to move into other positions and what is required in terms of skills and experience to qualify for them. This does not necessarily mean that a suitable position will be open at the time the employee has all required qualifications, but at least it show the possibilities and stimulates them to explore their options.

Determine a long-term career path for Highly Talented employees early on and focus on their career progression continually.
I call this the "Toyota Indonesia approach" as that is the organisation where I first heard about this. This method involves the company identifying High Potential talent early on and determining a target position in about two, five, eight or ten years' time and in that period promoting them towards that target.

The principle is that once talent is identified as Highly Talented, the company should determine what they see these people do after a number of years. Say there is potential in someone to become a VP after ten years then the plan should be to gradually promote the employee from his individual contributor position to Manager, Sr. Manager, Director and then VP. Others may be assessed to have their limits at a Director's level, in which case that should be the ultimate target.

The obvious issue here is that higher management positions don't easily come available. However, given headcount constraints, High Potentials should get absolute priority to other candidates to move into higher positions when they become available.

Career paths are a prerequisite for determining the target position in 5-10 years for High Potentials. It should be clear to employees what career progression they can make - this equally applies to non-Highly talented people, by the way. But for the talented employees it is an absolute prerequisite to establish a career path early in order to get them where they are envisaged to be. From each individual contributor position, there should therefore be paths defined throughout the organisation that broaden and deepen skills and experience – not only in the area of leadership, but also in other business areas than where the employee starts. Leaders should have a broad view of the company and not only be limited to their own department.

Manager, Employee, HR and others to identify or provide development opportunities

Once talent has been identified and a development plan created, the manager and employee should work on creating opportunities for the employee to gain relevant experience. These opportunities can come in the form of formal, existing (HR-organised) programmes, but may as well be initiated by the employee or manager themselves. What is important is that the highly talented employee gets the appropriate experience in the areas he needs to develop in. Make sure opportunities are not considered as free excursions, though: development opportunities need to be used to track progress in the desired areas and therefore the employee needs to be held accountable for making the most of the opportunity. If no relevant experience was gathered from an assignment it has been a waste of time.

Examples of development opportunities and the impact in an Integral sense are discussed in the following section.

Create a Feedback System

If not in place yet as part of the performance management system (see the previous chapter), talent management should use a 360-degrees feedback method where the highly talented employee is provided with feedback from people he has worked with in a certain period. Especially at the end of a particular assignment, feedback should be obtained to assess how the employee has done in the new context he has worked in, what the people he has worked with see as further development needs and what has gone well. This feedback system should be an integral part of the complete Talent Management system. Of course, the line manager and an independent mentor should provide this feedback as well.

Integrate the Talent Management System with Performance Management

Ideally, both Talent and Performance Management should take place on a continual basis. All too often, these are considered exercises that take place once or twice a year, but in reality, talent and performance should be constantly evaluated. Moreover, there is an obvious link between the two: talented people will more likely show high performance if they are given the right opportunities. In any case, they should be stimulated to perform beyond the usual requirements in order to develop themselves effectively. This implies that Talent and Performance Management should really be one system that focusses on developing the right people and holding them accountable for achieving their development and other targets. When doing so, a more integral way of dealing with employees' development is created through which everyone, not only the highly talented people, has the optimal chance to grow towards where they can and want to grow.

⁂

INTEGRAL OPPORTUNITIES FOR TALENT DEVELOPMENT

If we want to develop highly talented people fully, we need to look at them from all possible perspectives, i.e. in an integral way. Some practical opportunities to provide the employee with experience in all areas of the Integral Model are as follows. Note that all these experiences need to be tracked for their effectiveness in actually developing talent, with accountability primarily lying with the employee to benefit from the opportunities, but also with responsibility for the manager and HR to track development continually in the long term.

Job-rotation schemes
Full-time job-rotation may be difficult due to lack of backfill opportunities, therefore part-time may be more feasible.
Recently, I have set up a part-time job-rotation scheme between my department and Sales, where a manager from my team started working 50% as an Account Manager in Sales. This private initiative

may serve as an example for future initiatives, but should be more clearly supported by the company, in particular HR.

Job-rotation provides experience in the areas of organisational structure, the lower right corner of the Integral model.

Mentoring by an established leader

"Shadow a leader" or formal mentoring sessions. The company mentoring system has been around for many years, but it relatively unknown in EMEA. I have served as a mentor on many occasions, working with people from mostly North and South America. As a development tool, the mentoring system can be used very effectively, but needs properly prepared mentors, the right expectations from the mentees and further promotion by the company.

Mentoring provides opportunities to develop personal aspects such as attitude; identify knowledge gaps and assess behaviour, all aspects from the upper left and right quadrants of the Integral Model.

International Assignments

International assignments develop cultural awareness, an aspect of the lower left quadrant. In larger, international companies this is an aspect of work that cannot be underestimated: being able to work cross-culturally is a simple necessity to do business nowadays. So where possible, employees should be allowed to work in a different international location for a period of time, even if it is just a week or so. This has obvious financial implications, which, however, should pay themselves back in the true integral development of a highly talented employee.

Develop specific courses aimed at talented employees

I am rather sceptical about training, in particular about management training. As I already indicated in the introduction to this book, I am allergic to the old 1970's concepts that still seem to abound in management training courses. Moreover, often much of what is taught in the classroom is forgotten as soon as the usual daily routine starts again. However, in the many courses of this kind that I have attended, there were always the magical ten minutes that something did strike me and that I have been using as a valuable concept in the years after. It is these types of courses that should be developed for highly talented people. These employees should already be aware of SMART objectives, the Seven Habits and the emotional response of people to change. Courses for highly talented people should be tailored very specifically to their needs, so that they can learn what they most need. Furthermore, a high level of interaction and cooperation should take place during the training, with real-life situations where the employees can sharpen their skills and knowledge.

Training courses primarily work on the upper left (knowledge) and upper right (behaviour) quadrants of the Integral model, but, when set up in the right way, can also cover the lower two quadrants (cultural and organisational skills).

☐

WHY COACHING?

This chapter is about People Management, management of people. For some managers this is a necessary evil and for others instead a reason to go to work. In practice, people management may at times fall victim to the many other priorities managers have; priorities that are more closely aligned to business goals, for instance. In the end, bringing in a new contract or delivering a service on time for the customer is seen as more important that keeping the staff satisfied.

At the same time, it is impossible to achieve the latter things if those are not done by people in the company. The tacky slogan is that "people are our greatest assets" and however trite, it is true. A company consists of people doing their jobs and preferably doing their jobs *together*. "The customer" isn't an abstract phenomenon either, but consists of actual people as well. It is therefore necessary for every manager to be able to deal with people in an effective way and leveraging relationships with customer and with colleagues alike.

It is therefore important for all managers who have people report into them, but also for other people in a company, manager or not, who have regular contact with colleagues or customers (that is all of you, indeed) to have some people management skills. These skills lead to a team or an organisation that is motivated and satisfied and based on these qualities delivers the best they can. Motivation and achievements are after all closely aligned.

A good people manager has a lot in common with a good coach. As you know, I have a background in coaching and counselling, therefore I have applied many of the principles I learnt in those practices in my job as a manager as well. Note that a coach in this sense is not a psychotherapist – most managers are not qualified to deal with the psychological side of their staff and do interventions to help them solve their problems and should therefore stay far away from doing so. Even I never ever tried to be a therapist for the staff reporting to me, given that I wanted to have a separation between my role as a manager and my various other roles I could have towards people (for more details on confusion of these roles, see chapter 6). A coach is someone who knows how to guide people, knows how to set goals with them (even if these are not directly to do with company objectives, as we have seen in the chapter about Integral Performance Management) and foremost is a facilitator: he makes sure that his people have the tools and circumstances to do their job in the best way possible.

Note that a coach is in turn not a mentor: a mentor is someone who can be directive to people, based on their own experience in a specific field. Managers can be mentors, but not of their own people: this would confuse the role of coach/manager and that of a mentor. As we will see, my people management philosophy borrows from client-centred therapy, which has the premise that the client has all the resources available to him already to solve their problems. The role of the coach or therapist is to help him uncover those resources. Similarly so, the task of the people manager is to help the employees to uncover the resources they have to do their job in the best way possible. A people manager therefore doesn't need to be directive, but merely guiding.

The qualities of a good people manager are then similar to the qualities of a good coach. These can be summarised as follows:
- Communication
- Example behaviour
- Organisational insight
- Attitude

It won't be surprising to the attentive reader that these four aspects are derived from the four quadrants of the Integral Model. In the remainder of this chapter I will go into detail about what these aspects involve for the people manager, except for the last aspect, which is too important to the discussion and will be dealt with in a separate chapter.

COMMUNICATION

As noted in the introduction to this book, I have become interested in aspects of communication at the beginning of my career, when I was working as a consultant in various multinational companies in The Netherlands. I quickly noticed that a lack of communication was one of the main reasons why many processes did not run well. I had not found an explicit solution for this, though, until years later when I coincidentally got triggered by Neuro-Linguistic Programming (NLP). This is the only area where I do like a development from the 1970's, but, contrary to a lot of management-theory, NLP comes and goes in waves and has never really gotten accepted by a broad part of society. Perhaps it is because of the major misnomer of its name itself: NLP is little to do with Neurology, hardly to do with Linguistics and nothing to do with (computer) programming. Rather than that, NLP presents various models of language and communication that are useful for getting insight in your own way of communicating and that of others. The methods and techniques that NLP created came originally from coaching and psychotherapy, by observing how certain therapists became so successful in what they were doing. Obviously, the techniques derived from these observations were at first applied to psychotherapy itself. Later, however, they were applied in all sorts of areas, from negotiation to setting commercial goals and, as we will see, in people management as well.

This part of the chapter is therefore strongly based on NLP, without wanting to give a general primer on that subject (this primer is in fact available as Appendix C, for those interested). Rather than adding to the vast library of NLP-based books, I only use the most appropriate techniques for people management in this chapter, techniques of which I know they are most helpful for managers in their interaction with other people, be it their teams or others.

THE 8-STEP COMMUNICATION MODEL

Within NLP, the eight-step communication model (not to be confused with the 12-step model used by various organisations to help people off their addictions!) is the basis for everything someone wants to achieve with their communication, whether it is therapeutic, educational, project-related or coaching. On the one hand, the model can be used to set up communication in a proper way, by checking before a meeting that all eight steps are covered. On the other hand, it can be used to find the reason why communication did not work out and correct this in a future meeting.

In the following figure, the eight steps are shown. It may be clear, that the model really consists of seven steps and that the central position of Ecology as a permanent check during all steps is considered the eighth element. So the seven real steps are a cycle, which really starts with "Context," but can be spread across multiple meetings, so that stepping into the cycle can effectively be done at any point necessary. I will start our journey through the circle with Context, though, to have a logical beginning, but also because Context is the area where most problems in communication are located. From that point onwards, I will discuss various practical techniques from my interpretation and modification of NLP and other sources that are helpful for managers in their interaction with their employees.

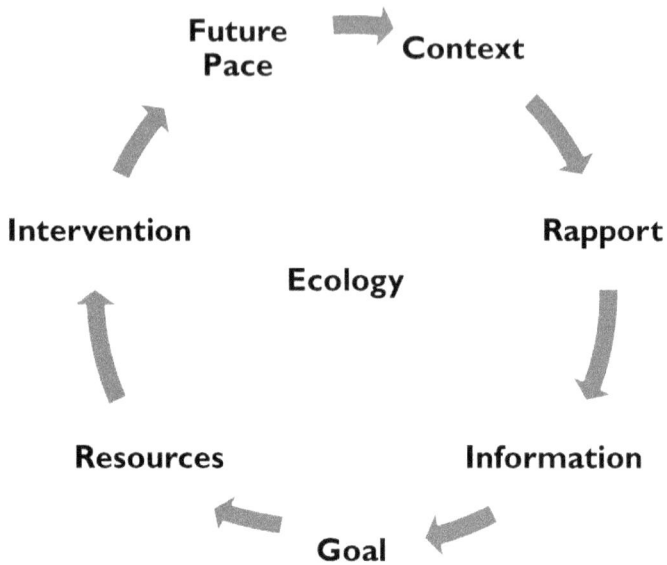

The 8-step communication model

STEP 1: CONTEXT

All communication ought to start with determining the framework or context within which the communication takes place. Why do a manager and his employee communicate, really? Is the understanding of the aim of this particular discussion or meeting the same with both or do the expectations around the aim differ? In practice it turns out that most misunderstandings have their origin here, because this first step of communication has not been agreed mutually, so that the people communicating each have a different goal in mind and eventually one of the two (or both) end up being disappointed, irritated or otherwise disgruntled, with the communication itself in fact having missed its aim completely.

Then what is it that we can do to make sure this first step, upon which the rest of the communication is based, is properly agreed? In the first place, this comes down to first "setting the frame," agreeing mutually what the meeting is about and what you are trying to achieve. This can be as simple as agreeing on a high-level agenda before the meeting, but can also get more complex when for instance a corrective action needs to take place after some incident happened. In the latter case, it needs to be clear what the corrective action's aim is, as people who made an error often expect to be punished in some way, which may not be the aim of their manager, who may just want to verify that the employee has learnt from his mistakes. Setting the frame also involves the mind-set of the participants: how do people think about certain subjects. As per the example, employees may think they will be punished for their mistakes whereas their managers just want to use them as a learning experience. Knowing each other's point of view and expectations on the subject at hand before the meeting is useful to make sure communication fulfils both people's intentions with it. Furthermore, the physical environment where communication takes place is of importance to set the context. Sensitive conversations should obviously not take place in the pantry where other people drink their tea, but rather in a private environment where you are not getting disturbed. I know of a company where one-to-one meetings would take place while walking around the campus (this was at a sports company), which gives a totally different dynamics to the meeting.

In short, setting the frame is about setting boundaries to what will be discussed and what not, thus agreeing on expectations of the communication so that both (or all, in the case of e.g. a team meeting) parties will know what the outcomes can and cannot be. This should lead to all participants having the feeling afterwards that the aim of the meeting has been fulfilled.

"Rapport" is a word that means tuning into each other: adjusting the means of expression so that there is a mutual understanding. When rapport is reached, there is a natural flow of communication between people that feels harmonised, without any difficulties. It creates a mutual trust and provides the possibility that people open up to each other because of that. Good rapport joins the two points of view in a one-to-one exchange and this in turn can create something new between people that may for example be the resolution of a conflict or the way forward in a situation that is to be solved. Building up rapport is a wide area within communication that has also been described thoroughly in NLP. I will deal with a number of subjects related to rapport in this section. These are Rapport itself, Models of the World and Perspectives.

Rapport

The constructive attitude between a manager and his employees is expressed with the word "rapport" in NLP. Rapport is the basis of the relationship between manager and employee. Rapport is within NLP also being explained as the relationship of mutual understanding, trust and agreement between people. It is the feeling that things run smoothly and naturally in all aspects of communication. At least, that is the somewhat more superficial definition of rapport. Because what is it exactly that causes this feeling? And what do you need to do to get there?

At a more fundamental level, rapport is about creating bonds between people. Those bonds can exist at four hierarchical levels: physical, emotional, mental and spiritual. These will lead to a more natural way of cooperating, which enhances effectiveness and productivity. One step further in this reasoning, the manager needs to be able to deal with all sorts of personal situations that the employee is dealing with, such as long-term sickness, death in the family, new-born children, etc. that will have an impact on work. Being able to empathise with the employee and being capable of fitting these situations into the job context demand from the manager that he can create a high level of rapport with the employee.

Starting at a **physical** level: this is the most basic level of rapport and it is generated by matching body-language. This body-language encompasses posture, movements, facial expressions and eye-contact between manager and employee. Making these physical aspects match, meaning that both parties use similar (not meaning the same) body-language during communication, creates a first bond between the two, which turns out to be favourable for mutual understanding. Experiment with it: notice how communication changes if you change from using similar postures, facial expressions and movements as the other to using different ones altogether. In NLP, the physical elements of rapport are understood to be: Head (i.e. facial expressions), Breathing, Posture, Tonality (of the voice), Speed (of speaking) and keeping Eye contact. These five mainly physical elements pave the way for the manager to creation of rapport with the employee.

Emotional rapport leads in the first instance to what is considered a "good feeling" between people and in a deeper sense to true empathy. This good feeling follows physical rapport and forms the basis of having a "pleasant conversation" between a manager and a staff member. Proper emotional rapport is more to do with *empathy*, though. Empathy goes far beyond the level of a pleasant conversation: it is about being able to be *touched* and *moved by* what the other is telling you and being able to express this back to him. Back in the days during my studies, I had difficulties getting to do the latter: even though I could feel for what someone was telling me about herself, I could typically not find the words to express this.

Until the moment that I heard a classmate use the following expression, "I can imagine that you had a hard time going through this." Since then, I have been able to use this phrase as a template for expressing my empathy successfully.

So empathy expresses an understanding of and compassion with the emotional situation of the other. To achieve this, you need a base perspective on the other's situation that goes a step beyond just physical rapport or having the feeling of a pleasant conversation. This perspective is to do with the core *attitude* of the manager, which shall be explained more deeply in a later chapter. For now, in the first place, the right attitude is about knowing your own emotions. If your own emotions have not developed very well (which happens a lot in the western world), it is hard to get in touch with them, harder to get a feeling for someone else's emotions, and fairly impossible to show empathy. Then no emotional bond between the manager and the employee can develop.

At a **mental** level it is said that you can have a good understanding with someone. The word "understanding" already indicates that this refers to the mental aspect of rapport: you maintain a bond that is rational, one that deals with thoughts, opinions and facts. This mental rapport is established by adjusting the use of language to that of the employee: people usually express themselves in specific ways (language patterns, preference for certain words or phrases, style, complexity, etc.). Adapting to those ways, without copying them explicitly, but by merely subtly mirroring the use of language by using similar words and expressions or following similar patterns of speech, leads to rapport at this mental level. In most companies, building rapport at this level is no issue at all, but do notice that mental rapport is to be built on top of physical and emotional rapport. Without those two as the basis, mental rapport misses its foundation en risks becoming an empty, because not truly sincere, shell.

Patterns of Language and Behaviour

The very beginning of NLP was formed by Richard Bandler and John Grinder, who observed several therapists and determined patterns in their language that seemed to be universal. This led to what they called the "Meta-model" of language. Apart from this, there are a number of smaller language structures that can be observed in the daily language used by all people.

The reason why it is useful to notice language patterns is that they reveal a person's experience of the situation. Language acts as a filter to our experience: you observe something (for example an object or event outside yourself or a feeling or thought inside yourself), which is processed by your senses (which is the first filter), which subsequently leads to the internal experience and then gets processed by the mind (the second filter) and expressed through symbolic sounds that we call language (third filter). The way in which you use language, specifically the patterns in your language, can therefore be used to go back to the original experience. Language expresses what you find, consciously or sub-consciously, important in that experience. Language patterns therefore give an indication of a deeper structure of your internal experience.

To make this more intuitive, here are two examples of a simple set of language patterns.

Firstly, there is a distinction between language that is visual, auditive, kinaesthetic or undetermined. Visual language uses words to do with seeing; auditive language uses words to do with hearing; kinaesthetic language uses words to do with feeling (physically). Undetermined language avoids using any of the previous and prefers abstract expressions. One and the same remark can then be expressed in four different basic ways, "The situation doesn't look good" (visual), "The situation doesn't sound right to me" (auditive), "The situation does not feel good" (kinaesthetic) or "The situation seems bad" (undetermined).

A second way of discerning language patterns is based on thinking, feeling and doing. Often people have a clear preference to express themselves in one of these three ways. They then express their own internal state (viz. their feelings), their external behaviour (or what they are doing) or their internal processes (their thoughts). At a basic level, people can then be distributed in thinkers, feelers and doers. A similar expression about my recent first-ever diving experience can then be expressed in these three different versions, "It was such a delightful experience, I felt completely free and happy" (internal state), "It was such an intense experience, I have done wonderful things" (external behaviour) or "It was a very interesting experience, I still think about it every day" (internal processes).

Beyond these simple models of language patterns is the *Meta Model*. This model made distinctions in a number of categories of language patterns: deletions, generalisations and distortions. Details about the Meta Model can be found in the NLP primer in Appendix C.

Finally, the highest level of rapport is the **spiritual** one. This level is the most comprehensive level of rapport that again goes a step further than physical, emotional and mental rapport. Mentioning anything "spiritual" often cause spontaneous panic-attacks with people in businesses, but it is more mundane than you would think. The spiritual level of rapport is to do with the basic attitude of the manager, which needs to reach a depth that constitutes a profound contact with himself, with the essence of his being, also known as his soul. Only when that contact has been established, rapport can be built between the manager's own spiritual aspects and those of the client. Later chapters, the ones about Leadership/Attitude and the final chapter will deal in more depth with this level.

The following figure shows the various levels of rapport as concentric circles: physical rapport is at the core or the base of all levels and is contained by emotional rapport. Emotional rapport in its turn is contained by mental rapport. And the all-embracing level of rapport is the spiritual one.

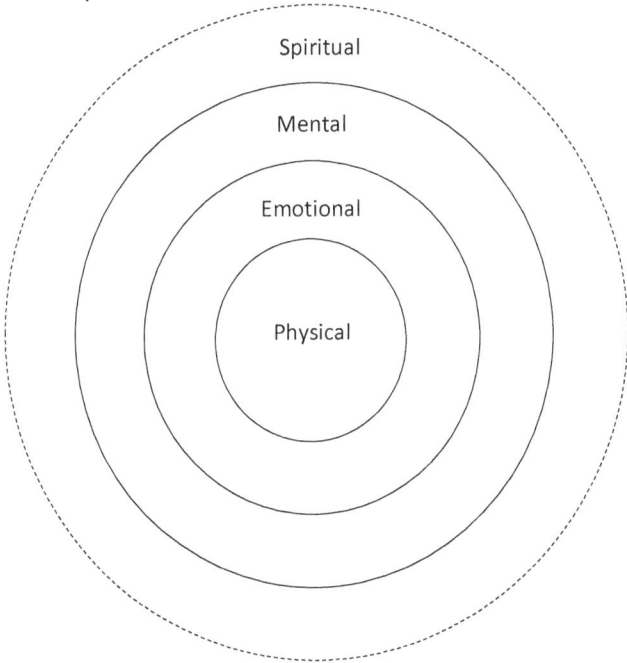

Spiritual

Mental

Emotional

Physical

Levels of Rapport

Models of the World

Something a manager should realise when communicating with employees is the fact that not everybody thinks in the same way, feels the same in similar situations or reacts and behaves in the same way. This is to do with the way in which every person has developed himself in the course of his life; this has led to certain preferences in the manner in which the world and reality around him are experienced and also how this experience is expressed in language. In the end this leads to a *Model of the World* that is unique to each individual and based on which people function differently. As a people manager you therefore need to take into account that your employees have, in the same situation, a different experience than you and will therefore react differently on things than you would react.

If you want to get an understanding of your staff, and a coaching manager does want that, then it is necessary to get insight into their Models of the World. A Model of the World consists of a number of elements, the most important ones of which are:

- *Values and Beliefs*: what is it that someone finds important in life and why is that?
- *Types*: what patterns can be found in someone's behaviour?
- *Levels of Development*: at what level of development is someone and how can you best deal with it as a manager?

Once you are aware of these things in your employees, you can adjust your approach to them accordingly. In the following three subsections, these elements will be discussed in more depth.

Values and Beliefs

Values are words that give a meaning to experiences and in that way provide a structure that causes us to want to repeat or avoid those experiences. This repetition or avoidance is a result of habit-formation, because we evaluate our experiences based on our values. For instance, an unpleasant experience such as an assault can be evaluated based on a value such as "Justice." If justice is important for us, then the experience of the assault will remain linked to that value and in turn will in a similar situation cause and emotion that is to do with infringement of our sense of justice, e.g. outrage.

Values are important because there is no communication as long as you don't know what is important to you and why you find that important. Goals are set by us in order to realise values: a value sich as "happiness" is for example one based on which you can set yourself many goals that try to fulfil that happiness. More in a business context, my current company has "shareholder value" high in its list of values and obviously strives to set corporate objectives aligned with that value.

Values don't exist in isolation of other values: there is a hierarchy of values for everyone, where some values are deemed more important than others and vice versa. Also, values can be deemed equally important and be combined to lead to higher values. This hierarchy is very much dependent on the individual preferences and level of development. Therefore, the hierarchy of values forms an important part of someone's Model of the World.

A *belief* is a general statement about oneself or the world, of which one is convinced that it is true. So a statement such as "shareholders are important to us" becomes a belief if someone starts to be convinced that this is the truth. Beliefs are built around values (in this case, "shareholder value") and are rules that are made in order to fulfil or avoid certain values. A belief is first and foremost an assumption, though, meaning that it is something you assume is true in order to understand what is happening around you. Once the assumption is confirmed often enough, it will turn into a belief.

Beliefs can also be limiting to someone's functioning: in this case, the belief is impeding the path to achieving a goals. For example, if we believe that managers are evil, our goal to make promotion in the company will be blocked by that belief.

If needed, a limiting belief can be neutralised. The best way to do so is to let someone feel the opposite of their belief, preferably multiple times. Doing so, the limiting belief will lose its strength and will disappear eventually, being replaced by a more constructive belief.

Types
Different people have different preferences and react differently when they are in the same situation. One of the reasons for this is that during our lives, certain patterns of preferences develop themselves in the areas of thinking, acting and experiencing. Those patterns have been classified by various researchers in different ways (according to their own patterns of preference!) and resulted in what can be generically called "Types." Well-known type classifications are those of Myers-Briggs (sixteen different types), the Enneagram (nine types) and NLP has defined its own Meta-programmes (sixty variations). Going into detail is beyond the scope of this book, but can be found easily on the Internet or in literature (see the references list at the end of this book for some suggestions).

In practice, these types give some more insight in how an employee prefers functioning (even if he is unaware of it himself), which increases understanding of why he tends to act in a certain way. It is this understanding that can lead the manager to build more rapport with the employee.

Do take care with types, though, because all too often they are used in a sense of saying "I *am* a Myers-Briggs ISTJ type" as if there is nothing else to say about a person. These sorts of statements are in fact *stereotypes* rather than statements about how someone functions. They lead to classifying people into easy categories and assuming that everyone in a category is the same. This is not the case. Types tell you something about the surface structure of people's behaviour, not about who they are in depth. The deeper structure of a person's behaviour and psychology is more to do with levels of development than types, which is what we are going to deal with next. This deeper structure needs to be understood by a manager as well to get to the next level of rapport with his staff.

Levels of Development

Next to the aforementioned Types that give a surface-description of someone's preferences, the more (psychologically) deeply located *Levels of Development* also play an important role. Development can take place in all sorts of areas, as indicated in the chapter about Performance Management. In this topic we are, however, referring to the psychological development of an employee. In that area there are various models, of which the one developed by Abraham Maslow (the hierarchy of needs) is probably the best-known. All those psychological models of development are very similar when compared to each other, though. As we already described in the first chapter, levels of development can be used to understand psychological characteristics of people. People grow from birth to a certain level of development and then either stay there when they are adults or continue to grow until the end of their lives.

Depending on the model used, we can distinguish anywhere between five to fifteen levels of development. These levels can be radically simplified into three rough categories, though, depending on what is considered "conventional" or "common." People who are at a level of development that is called "conventional" like to comply with rules and regulations and feel safest in a pre-determined role. They follow the rules of a company and comply with social values and norms. Prior to this, people are at a "pre-conventional" level: these people are more focussed on themselves and show somewhat egocentric behaviour. But there are also people who can be called "post-conventional," who acknowledge the importance of following group rules, but are also looking for flexibility and alternatives to stimulate their own progress and development. Rules and roles may be in the way of those goals.

These three broad categories of people will all act differently and take decisions in a different way. As a manager you better be aware of this, because you need to approach these people in different ways as well. Each category of people needs a different approach and if you combine your insight in these levels of development with your insight in the various types, you get to a whole range of characterisations that make individual people unique. That is the reason why relationships between a manager and individual employees need to be set up differently for different people as well.

Perspectives

A *perspective* in the communication between two or more people can be seen as the point of view from which someone observes the situation or, in popular verbiage, "where he comes from." This perspective has great influence on the way in which a situation is experienced. Looking at a situation from our own perspective is often easy, because that is what we usually do all day long anyway, but it is often very enriching to also look at the situation from someone else's perspective or from a neutral point of view.

NLP defines four perspectives, also referred to as *positions*, which are clarified in the following figure.

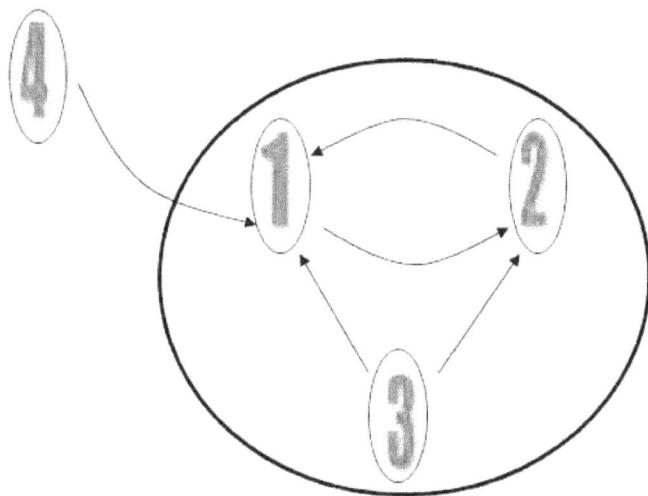

Perspectives. The first and second positions are in communication with each other. The third position is a neutral observer. The fourth position is an observer of the first position.

First Perspective: in the first perspective, everything is experienced from the own point of view. The world is looked at from your own vantage point and expressed in your own language patterns. There is no place for someone else's perspective. This is not meant negatively, because this first position is also the only one in which you can experience your reaction to what the other tells you, where you can be *touched* by what is happening around you or what someone else is doing or saying.

Second Perspective: in the second perspective the world is experienced from the position of the other. This is also a fruitful position to take, because doing some efforts to understand the experience of the other and feel what he feels leads to a level of empathy. As mentioned before, empathy is about being able to share someone else's feelings and expressing what that does with you (the latter being a function of the first position) and being able to give that back verbally to the other. In the second perspective, you are effectively trying to make the other's perspective your own in order to get a better understanding of him.

Third Perspective: this perspective is often referred to as the Meta-position or simply Meta (from the Greek word μετά meaning "beyond" and in English often translated as "about"). This is the helicopter-view of things, a neutral observer of positions 1 and 2. Note that in order to be Meta, you need to have been in positions 1 and 2 first and empathise with those. The third perspective has a similar distance to position 1 and 2, so is impartial, but at the same time acts as an honest observer of what is taking place between positions 1 and 2. It is a neutral perspective on what happens in the communication between 1 and 2 and in that way has an evaluating function that helps to take a step back and look at the situation objectively.

Fourth Perspective: this is a Meta that only observes position 1. Here we are an observer of ourselves and how we function in a situation. In the best sense, this is a reflection on your own performance, a neutral assessment of what you are doing. In the worst case, though, this can end up in a continuous judging of yourself, always being critical of everything you do. It may be like having someone look across your shoulder all the time, but that person being yourself. If we can avoid these negative aspects of being in the fourth position, it becomes possible to evaluate ourselves and to see how we are functioning, what is going well and what can be improved in our acting and communicating.

In the end, when you are working with an employee you need to be able to look at the situation from as many perspectives as possible, at least from your and his perspectives. Only then can you get a complete view of the situation and learn to understand how it is really structured.

STEP 3: INFORMATION

The previous two steps had as their goals to get the proper alignment between the manager and the employee within the agreed context. Once this has been established, it is time from that position to actually get a grasp of what the issue is that the employee wants to discuss (or what the employee thinks of the issue that you want to discuss). This means that information needs to be gathered.

DIKW

Rather than *information*, we need to gather *data* (which is the raw input you get from the employee), which can be processed into intelligible information (which is a structured set of data answering questions about the "who," "what," "when," and "where" of this situation, so adding context to data). Conclusions drawn from information then lead to actual *knowledge* about the situation; this adds experiences, ideas, insights, values and beliefs to information. Knowledge paired with your experience and broader awareness of the context ultimately leads to *wisdom*, which is what you should base your conclusions and decisions on. This small hierarchy of knowledge management is based on an ever-growing *understanding* of the issues and interpretation of the *context*. In summary, it is referred to as the Data-Information-Knowledge-Wisdom or DIKW structure. NLP refers to step 3 as "Information," but should really refer to "Wisdom" if the right results are to be obtained in communication. For the purpose of continuity I will stick to the word "Information" in this section, though.

What do we need to gather relevant information? The main thing to do is to simply *listen*. This should not be very surprising, but the question is, what listening well involves exactly. Listening well starts

103

with a good *rapport* (which is why that step comes before this one). In addition to building rapport, listen requires you to give *space* to the employee and asking the right follow-up *questions*.

Rapport we dealt with extensively in the previous sections. Creating space is a matter of opening yourself up to what the employee wants to tell you en giving him time to express himself without interrupting him, except in the case when you really need clarification. By no means insert your own opinion into the speech of someone else (this is one of the more irritating things I encounter in meetings, especially when many people are present). Only interrupt when something is not immediately clear to you. Do not draw conclusions yet before the other is done, let alone start giving advice. This can wait until the end, if the employee cannot solve the issue with his own resources. Once he is finished speaking, you can dig into it and ask follow-up question in order to get further clarification on things. This will lead to a dialogue that provides both the manager and the employee sufficient insight into the problem and enables both of them to set goals to solve it. The next step deals with making that goal more specific.

STEP 4: GOALS

Literally every management book or training has a section about setting goals (also known as Objectives or Critical Success Factors/Key Performance Indicators) and using the SMART acronym to do this, so I am not going to go into that. Goals are after all a well-known and necessary phenomenon in companies, mostly in a financial-economic sense. A company exists thanks to achieving a certain net result and formulating and achieving goals are a necessary periodic activity to do so. Goals give direction to the work that needs to be done and stimulate cooperation within the organisation.

When coaching an employee, it will also be necessary to agree on certain goals in the area if his functioning. The chapter about Integral Performance Management has gone into detail about a method to do so already, including the use of the NLP Outcome Frame to describe goals that are not explicitly quantitatively measurable.

A step beyond formulating an objective is determining why you find it important to achieve that objective. This is related to values and beliefs and can indeed be described as such. If, for instance, you have formulated a goal with your employee that deals with him learning to communicate more effectively with other people, then the associated belief can be that good communication is a prerequisite for true teamwork and that through good teamwork, the productivity (which can be considered a value) is improved as well. Beliefs and values associated with objectives strengthen the objectives and make it more likely that the employee will actually achieve them.

STEP 5: RESOURCES

Resources are the skills, knowledge and qualities that an employee already has, but are not necessarily available to him to use in practice. From a psychological point of view, NLP says that everyone already has all resources available to solve their own problems. They merely need guidance from their manager to use those resources effectively. This obviously does not always apply to knowledge and practical skills, which are resources that can be acquired or developed.

Existing resources can be used by the employee to solve issues, provided the resources have been developed sufficiently. A technical problem can only be solved if the skills and knowledge are available at the right level; a company-political problem can be tackled if the skills in the strategic and communicative areas are at a high enough level.

If the required resources are not available or have not been developed well enough, Integral Performance Management can oave the way to get them at the right level – see the earlier chapter for an extensive description of this method.

If resources seem to be missing altogether, it may be necessary for the manager to intervene in order to either activate those resources or find alternatives. The next step in the communication model is therefore the step where interventions can be used.

I fan employee is not able to achieve goals, as agreed in step 4 of the communication model, by himself, for instance because the necessary resources are not available or cannot be developed, then it is necessary for the manager to get actively involved. This involvement or intervention (which literally means "getting in between") can lead to the resources the employee needs becoming available, so he can then proceed and handle the situation himself.

This kind of interventions does not need to be complex, let alone therapeutic in nature. In fact, from the list that follows, a number of interventions will already be known. Others may be new or may have to be left to specialists. An overview of some possible interventions is as follows.

Environment:
- Making sure that the employee can continue to function in the company environment and contributes sufficiently to it.

Behaviour:
- Training in the area of practical skills;
- Performance Management (see the earlier chapter);
- Awarding good behaviour and achieving goals or discussing/punishing if this is not the case.
- Stimulating and improving communication skills.
- Adjusting behaviour such that the employee can deal with his colleagues constructively in the existing environment.

Emotions:
- Solving emotionally blocking issues that are in the way of doing a good job.

- Preparing the team for major change in the organisation.
- Balancing emotions such that the right behaviour for the work environment can be achieved.

Capabilities:
- Education in the areas of knowledge and skills;
- Coaching for being able to effectively us existing knowledge and skills.
- Using knowledge and skills to be able to deal more effectively with change and emotional issues.

Beliefs and Values:
- Doing a contrast analysis of the values and beliefs of the employee versus those of the company; trying to align the two.
- Assess the employee's professional needs and looking to fulfil those.
- Based on these values, beliefs and needs determine the required capabilities to fulfil them and do a good job.

Role:
- Determine the most appropriate role for the employee and adjust it if necessary.
- Based on the current role, see what needs, values and beliefs of the employee and of the company are associated with it and make sure they can be fulfilled.

Identity:
- Determine what motivates or inspires the employee.
- Use this motivation as a baseline for determining the right role within the organisation.

Logical Levels

The previous list of interventions is not a random one, but was based on the *Logical Levels* originally conceived by Gregory Bateson and modified by Robert Dilts, Eric Schneider and myself. The Logical Levels (also known as Logical Orders) have become a standard part of

---

NLP and show a hierarchy of things that have an influence on how people function in a certain situation. The higher the level, the greater the influence on the situation, because higher levels influence lower levels in the model. The following figure is the basic model of Logical Levels.

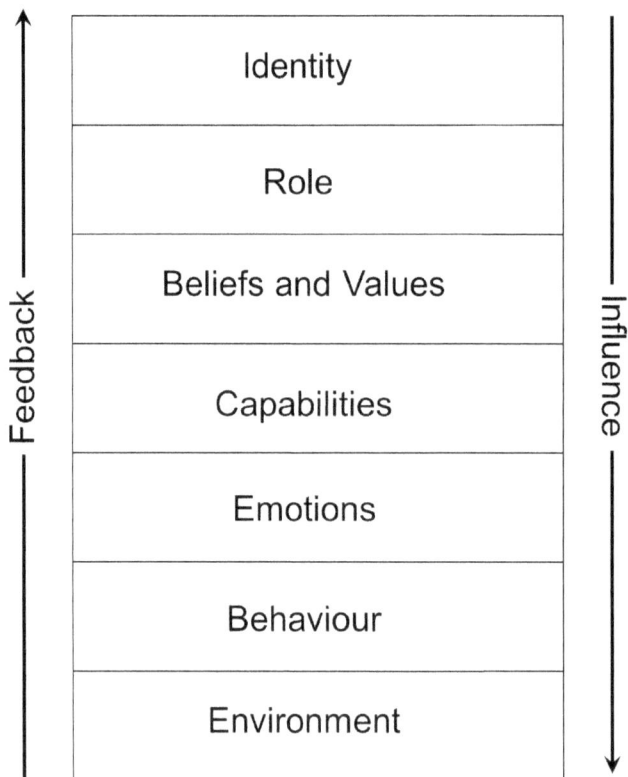

Identity
Role
Beliefs and Values
Capabilities
Emotions
Behaviour
Environment

Feedback ↑ (left axis) — Influence ↓ (right axis)

Logical Levels (after Bateson, Dilts, Schneider and Van der Haven)

For example, the behaviour of an employee has a direct influence on his colleagues and work environment. Inversely, the lower levels provide feedback to the higher levels: how we function at a lower level indicates if something may need to be adjusted at the level above or not. An employee who is in the wrong role will therefore have to look at what actually motivates him (at Identity level) before another, more suitable role, can be found.

A brief explanation of the hierarchy of the Logical Levels is as follows. *Behaviour* is above the impact it has on the Environment or Context, because the effect is influenced by the behaviour. Our activities have a certain effect in the situation (or environment) that we are in. Inversely, the environment gives us feedback on our behaviour: in this way, our behaviour can be considered to be good or evil based on the effect it had on the environment.
Emotions are close to behaviour, as our emotional state all-too-easily determines how we behave. Behaviour of ourselves and others in turn provide feedback at an emotional level based on which we can modify our behaviour.
Our *capabilities* influence our emotional state and in that way the choices we make for our behaviour – therefore capabilities influence our emotions and behaviour and are positioned on top of it.
Our *Beliefs and Values* indicate how and what we think about ourselves, what we believe in, what we think is important. The reality of what we observe around us is a reflection of what we believe in. Therefore, we can say that our Values and Beliefs influence our Capacities. At the same time, capacities give feedback about our values and beliefs and may indicate that it is time to change those. Quite some NLP procedures work at this level, where capacities and beliefs interact.
If there are values and beliefs, then there must be something that organises them and creates order among them. In the first place, this is the *Role* that we are in, specific to the job that we are doing. Wider

than this specific role, however is *Identity*. Identity is what we are, that of which we say, "I Am." Role is a subset of this Identity. Identity influences, determines and uses the values and beliefs and at the same time our values and beliefs are a reflection of our Identity.

For the manager it is important to determine at what logical level an issue is located; once this is known, it can be seen what kind of intervention may be needed that has an effect at that level.

* * *

A Practical (and Personal) Example

While writing the above section, it occurred to me that I have recently applied these principles to myself. The fact is that I had chosen to give up my position as a Senior Manager because the demands of the job and the direction given by my management made me unhappy. I have taken a step into a different area, still related to my previous job, and have created a position that makes me much happier. Without going into specific details, I applied the Logical Levels from the top down and came to the following self-assessment and associated interventions.

Identity: As stated above, the nature of my job as a Sr. Manager became such that it made me unhappy. More fundamentally, it meant that I was asked to do and be involved in things that went against my judgment, values and which I could not defend to myself or others.

Role: Changing roles from Sr. Management to (now) first-line management and leaving behind the organisation that I helped building for years was a big step. At the same time, it allowed me to find a new role and I was left free to fill it in myself.

Beliefs and Values: The beliefs that were in question were to do with how I wanted to deal with my organisation and with the people in it. Moreover, what measures overall are good for the organisation and how do you balance the needs of the organisation and those of the people in it? These were issues where I could not match my own beliefs and values (such as personal integrity and the well-being of

110

the people) with those of the larger organisation. In my new job, which still has a lot to do with my previous organisation, these clashes of beliefs and values are far more remote and outside my direct responsibility. Hence, my current position is one that fits me much better at this logical level.

Capabilities: Taking what I call an auto-demotion did not necessarily mean that I went down a level in required skills as well. On the contrary, I have stepped into areas where I needed new skills and could put into practice knowledge that I had not been able to put into practice before.

Emotions: It is clear to me that I feel much happier in my current job. People around me notice this as well. This had a great impact on my life, where I could be truly depressed, also outside work. That is all gone now. Also gone is the fear of starting something new and undefined (I created something similar to an outcome frame for my new job, which helped) as well as the fear of being made redundant (which did not happen).

Behaviour: Due to my being happier in my job and being relieved of pressures that I did not want to deal with, I feel my productivity at work as well as privately has increased (this book being a result of it!). I feel happier in my dealings with people around me and am more energetic now.

Environment: I decided to move out of my office at work and be among other people again, which is fantastic. I needed that office to be able to discuss things privately, but was not fully happy being alone all day either. So the interaction with people around me, without being constantly disturbed either, works well for me and for the people I work with.

STEP 7: FUTURE PACE

Prior to the communication circle ending, it needs to be verified how things are going to run in the future. This is on the one hand a check of the individual steps in the planning that has been made based on

111

e.g. an outcome or interventions. We need to verify whether the activities and the timing thereof are realistic and manageable. On the other hand, it is also a possibility in this step to have the employee imagine in a detailed way what the situation will be like in the future once all agreed steps have been taken. This has an even better impact if it is described in writing. Will there still be a problem in the future (in which case another round of the communication cycle may need to be started in order to tackle any remaining problem) or is he much better equipped to deal with the issues at hand? This check of the future, in NLP referred to as Future Pace, is at the same time a quality check to assess the whole communication and coaching process and see if there are any loose ends left to handle before the conversation is completed. If there are any open ends, as indicated, we can start the cycle from the start again (defining the Context) and continue along the same steps as before.

STEP 8: ECOLOGY

Within practically all environments I consider Ecology as one of the most fundamental aspects that need to be kept in mind at all times in order to deal with other people in a proper manner. In the eight-step communication model, Ecology is therefore not an individual step, but it is an aspect that plays a role in each of the seven other steps so we can verify that the employee, the manager, the company and the environment in which we work are not harmed by what we do, but benefit from our activities.

The word "ecology" is used in various ways by various people, which obviously leads to confusion about what the concept precisely involves. In practice, the following three definitions can be discerned: the classical one, the NLP one and the Integral one.
The *classical* definition of ecology is the one we all know from biology and from the environmental movements. In this definition, ecology is part of the branch of biology that studies the relationships between

various animals and plants and their environment. Going a step further, the concept of ecology is explained as the environment and everything in it, more specifically the preservation of it. Ecological agriculture and ecological stores are an example of this. Somewhat further along this line of thought, also all the production methods of food, the transport of it and the social circumstances of the farmers are part of ecology. This classical definition therefore is mainly concerned with the biosphere, that is, the whole of living beings and their environment. It is that biosphere that requires preservation in this classical definition.

The *NLP* definition of ecology is somewhat different from the classical one, for it is not only aimed at the biosphere, but at man as a whole. According to the NLP definition, ecological behaviour involves preventing doing harm to yourself, to others or to the environment. This definition needs to be honoured in every act of the therapist in relationship with his client. Ask yourself the following questions. What is the (positive) intention of the act? What are possible side-effects and can those side-effects have a negative impact? Is the client's welfare served with this act? Are there any ethical consequences? In this definition, ecology boils down to having respect for the other and to making sure that everything you do is in the interest of the other. Note that in all this, the ecological interest of the therapist needs to be kept in mind as well. Similarly to the client's ecology, the therapist's ecology is of central importance as well. After all, it makes little sense to help the other and at the same time cause harm for oneself.

The third, *integral* definition of ecology goes beyond these first two definitions and looks at man as not only part of the biosphere, i.e. as a living being among living beings, but also as part of the "*noosphere*," i.e. man should at a mental level be seen as part of an interactive whole of minds (nous is Greek for mind). A movement that calls itself Deep Ecology uses a definition of ecology that is effectively the classical on extended with the noosphere. However, extending this, you can also say that the noosphere is itself part of the *"theosphere,"* which is the spiritual sphere of influence of which all living beings are part. This spiritual sphere of influence is identified by Spirit, which is the ground from which all life originates and to which all life evolves (more about this can be read in the final chapter). Note also, that these various spheres are *holonic* in nature: the biosphere includes the geosphere of all matter; the biosphere itself is incorporated by the noosphere; the noosphere in turn is incorporated by the theosphere. So this last definition of ecology practically states that no harm should be done to yourself or someone else at the physical, emotional, mental of spiritual levels. In that way, human life is included in all its aspects. As long as all those aspects are protected in everything we do, we can truly say that we are acting ecologically.

EXAMPLE BEHAVIOUR

Next to Communication, a second aspect of the people manager is his own behaviour, more specifically related to the fact that necessarily, a manager needs to show example-behaviour. He is observed by many of his team members for the right way to do things, whether he wants it or not and whether that is justified or not. A team will very often model the manager's behaviour and adjust their own behaviour accordingly. A manager who cuts corners himself will not inspire his team to work hard. It is therefore senseless, if not hypocritical, to demand things from your team that you don't do yourself. "Walking the talk" is a saying that is very much applicable in this case. This expresses itself in work hours, overtime, taking breaks or not, personal development activities, etc. This example-function can also be seen in a more integral way: apart from the manager's behaviour, aspects from the other quadrants have an example function as well, such as attitude (upper left), social interests (lower right) and cultural awareness (lower left). A good example gets many followers.

Does this imply that the manager needs to be Mr. Perfect? In fact, it does, up to a point, if you want to maintain a level of credibility as a manager. However, there is consensus that Mr. Perfect does not exist and the team is aware of that as well and will be forgiving for mistakes. Do be aware of the fact that the higher the position, the more visibility there is of how people at that position function and negative aspects are gladly discussed at the coffee-machine at work. The other day I was having lunch with some of my team members and I made a joke saying that I was well aware that people were talking about me behind my back. Some of the team members looked at me and started laughing in a way that gave away that this was indeed the case, so they confirmed my suspicions about what was going on. Be therefore aware of how people look at you, that they have certain implicit expectations of you as their manager and that they will adapt their behaviour to the behaviour and attitude you show in hour work.

ORGANISATIONAL INSIGHT

In a true integral manner, the way in which a company is structured has a big influence on its culture and the well-being of the people working for it and therefore on their behaviour. For example: an unnecessarily hierarchically structured company in which hardly any decisions can be made without having to escalate to a couple of management layers above, leads to inefficiencies and as a result to low productivity. More importantly, it demotivates people and this decreases productivity even more. The question is therefore, how as a manager you set up your organisation in such a way that the employees in it can perform in an optimal manner. The criteria for it can be derived from the influence that "organisation" as a phenomenon in the lower right quadrant has on aspects from the other quadrants, viz. productivity (upper right), culture (lower left) and motivation (upper left).

The role of the manager in this aspect is very much that of a facilitator: you need to build the environment in such a way that the people in it can do their jobs as best as possible. This involves that all unnecessary overhead needs to be avoided. There is a balance there: on the one hand, a certain amount of control is needed to measure output and goal achievement. On the other hand, putting too many checks and balances into place creates a bureaucracy that actually reduces productivity rather than stimulates it. Overhead can also consist of having too many meetings in place, which are often caused by too large a distribution of responsibilities across different organisations, necessitating continual meetings to agree on interfaces or cooperation. Also, too large a number of databases and systems to work with to gather the required information for daily activities leads to unnecessary overhead. Furthermore, as mentioned before, having to wait for higher management decisions rather than being empowered to take those decisions at a lower level is not a structure that enhances productivity. Minimising these kinds of dependencies facilitates an efficient work environment for the employees.

Another aspect of organisation is how you build your team. Of course, every manager wants to have the most qualified people in his team, but the question is, whether that also means that these people can cooperate well. Will there not be any internal conflicts, character clashes and will the team be balanced in a way that overall satisfaction and productivity are optimal? These considerations point to the fact that when putting a team together you need to take into account what the backgrounds are of all individuals in there and whether these match when people need to cooperate. That said, it would be ideal if you can start hiring people for a team from scratch, so that you can adapt all people to each other, but in practice teams shape themselves in the course of time, get merged, split up, moved around, so that you will not always have a choice when it comes to picking the right people. However, do make the assessment of each team member, whether they are existing or new, in terms of their character and use the Types and Levels of Development to get some insight into their preferred behaviour patterns.

CROSS-CULTURAL MANAGEMENT

Finally, a bit about culture. Western societies are nowadays composed of people whose origins stem from many different cultural and national backgrounds. This can also be noticed in work environments: about eight years ago, I led a team of more than 40 employees, with at least 15 different cultures or nationalities. I never experienced issues with this, even though this seems to be an inviting environment for culture clashes. On the contrary, I have discovered a number of, sometimes very practical, benefits. For instance, the Portuguese people tended to start working pretty late for Dutch standards (between 11 and 12 am), but did work on until 8 or 9 pm, so could cover late activities. Also, some people with a Muslim background did not care much about Christian holidays, so they were fine working on Christmas and Easter. In exchange, I was happy to give them a few days off at the end of Ramadan.

Apart from these practical considerations, having a cross-cultural team also has the benefit that it generates radically different insights on various issues. This in itself is immediately the great challenge of managing people with various cultural backgrounds: the reconciliation of all those perspectives, values and beliefs into one whole that works for the complete organisation.

The main step to take when managing people with a different cultural background than your own is to let go of all your preconceptions or even prejudices about who they are. Not all Hindus are made equal and neither are all Bulgarians. Stereotypes do have a core of truth to them (yes, many Hindus do perform all sorts of mystical rituals on important life events and yes, 78% of Bulgarians don't play a lot of sports), but you will undoubtedly run into people that do not match the stereotypes. So put the stereotypes away and look at the person in front of you. You will indeed see some things that fit a larger cultural group, but you will see as many, if not more, things that are unique to that person. Especially if you use some of the NLP techniques that have been explained earlier in this chapter, you will be able to discern all those unique aspects of people that make them different from the everyday Hindu or Bulgarian that you might have expected. Overcoming preconceptions mean in the first place realising that you do have them – this is nothing to be ashamed of, it rather is something that all of us have developed as a way of coping with everything around us, making sense of things, putting things in patterns and categories to be able to handle them. The next step is putting yourself into the shoes of the other (second position) and realising what preconceptions and prejudices do to them exactly. Finally, look at them as unique individuals as described above, and see them as the persons that they are, removed from any stereotypes, preconceptions and generalisations. People are far more complex than what stereotypes tell you, so appreciate that complexity. The more you really put your interest in them, the more you will realise that they are so much different from the simplistic stereotypical notions we learn from certain areas of society and certain media.

In general, bringing the perceived cultural differences together into a single varied whole will enable organisations to grow healthier, wealthier and wiser.

Once you have stepped beyond the cultural stereotypes, you can focus on the other aspects of your employees, focussing on the aspects that do matter for forming a team that cooperates well and contributes significantly to the goals of the organisation.

I will be brief about attitude in this chapter, because the complete next chapter is devoted to it. The attitude, or base stance and perspective of the manager towards others, is crucial in his communication with people. It impacts rapport and example behaviour and lies at the basis of his leadership capabilities. This is why the next chapter, which is nominally about leadership, will deal in the core with attitude and will explain what it is and how we can use it to benefit out leadership qualities.

To be honest, I am sick and tired of the word "leadership."
And it's all the fault of people like me writing management books.

I guess you will understand me if you, like me, have read book after book, attended seminar after seminar, participated in a score of courses and got hammered with all sorts of lousy definitions of what leadership is supposed to be. And in the end, do you really know what it is?

Apologies in advance, but here is another attempt to get to a true definition of leadership, albeit seen from a different perspective than is usually taken. That is the only reason why I believe I have something new to add to the discussion.

Leadership is the number one buzz-word in management circles and the subject of a great many books, courses and seminars. Similar to many other subjects in this area, nobody really agrees (or cares) about a proper definition of leadership. The only agreement is the fuzzy notion that a manager requires leadership skills, without going into any detail about what that means.
Below are a number of definitions from a couple of sources that deal with management leadership.

Leadership is the capacity to initiate action without the use of force or fear. Great leaders think, listen and speak in a way that energizes people to give more than is required to produce more than what is expected. When that critical margin of discretionary effort is accessed, what seemed impossible becomes possible and what seems possible becomes real.
(Pacific Integral Leadership)

Leadership is a relational term—it identifies a relationship in which some people are able to persuade others to adopt new values, attitudes and goals, and to exert effort on behalf of those values, attitudes and goals. The relationship is almost always configured by and played out within the parameters of a group—a small group like a team, a medium-sized group like an organization, or a large group like a nation. The values, attitudes and goals that leaders inspire others to adopt and to follow are ones that define and serve the group—and thus leaders are able to transform individual action into group action.
(Michael A. Hogg – Social Identity and Leadership)

Leaders provide vision and direction to their followers. They provide answers to the questions, "Where are we going? What are our objectives? What are we trying to achieve?"
(David M. Messick - On the Psychological Exchange between Leaders and Followers)

Sigmund Freud's (1921) Group Psychology and the Analysis of the Ego offers a fascinating and surprisingly broad account of leadership. It includes the ideas that groups have an instinctive need for leadership, and that individuals whose personal qualities are strong and prototypical, and whose ideas are compelling, are likely to succeed as leaders. It argues that followers have strong emotional attachments to leaders, even though these attachments may contain some ambivalence. It holds that fair treatment by leaders is key to producing obedience.
(George R. Goethals – The Psychodynamics of Leadership)

The problem with these definitions is that they are all written at a level of abstract concepts such as *Vision, Direction, Capacities* and *Values*. What leadership means concretely and in practical terms does not become any clearer.

It will not surprise you that the concept of Leadership can be interpreted in a much broader way than the classic definitions do once we apply the Integral Model to it. That is exactly what I am going to do in this chapter and I will add two ideas to it that are instrumental in keeping everything together: the *attitude* of the leader and the *ecology* that needs to be taken into account at all times.

When we take a tour through the Integral Model in the context of leadership, we end up with a couple of perspectives as depicted in the following figure and described in detail below.

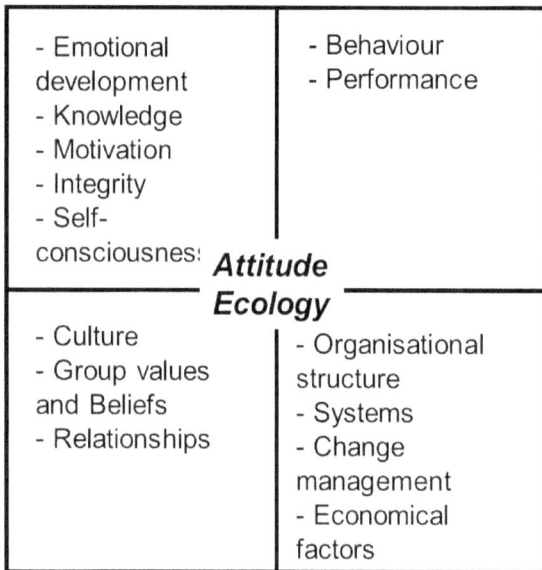

- Emotional development - Knowledge - Motivation - Integrity - Self-consciousness	- Behaviour - Performance
Attitude	
Ecology	
- Culture - Group values and Beliefs - Relationships	- Organisational structure - Systems - Change management - Economical factors

Figure 1. Integral Leadership.

122

Upper Left: the focus in this quadrant is on achieving personal excellence at the emotional (knowing your own feelings and being able to express empathy for other people's feelings), rational (knowledge), motivational (why do I like what I am doing) and spiritual (self-consciousness, personal mission, purpose of your role as a leader) levels. Leadership starts with getting to know yourself in all these areas and then being able to put them to use effectively.

Upper Right: here we are looking at the behaviour and the performance of the leader. What are the effects of the manager's activities and does he achieve his goals doing so? A leader knows how to adjust his behaviour to his environment and to the context in which he works. The context is about the company itself, the people who work in it, the customers and the corporate objectives. This context needs adjustment of external behaviour and a proper assessment of the impact of the manager's behaviour on this environment.

Lower Left: this side is about optimally organising your own team or organisation or the company as a whole – this requires insight into the effects of certain organisation structures (e.g. hierarchical versus flat) on the people and on cooperation with the customers. A hierarchical organisation is not always the right choice and neither is a flat one. Systems used in a company for e.g. ERP, CRM, time booking or service portfolio management are as much of an influence on the functioning of a company. They can influence work both positively and negatively, depending on these systems achieving the desired efficiency improvement or not. Finally, the external economic factors are important influences on being able to reach the financial and economic objectives of the company. Leadership in this quadrant means that the manager is a master in tuning all these aspects in order to achieve his goals.

Lower Right: the culture of the organisation has a great impact on the well-being of the employees in it. There are sufficient stories about people who have left a company because they did not like the working atmosphere. It can therefore be easily imagined that creating a positive culture in a team or rather in the company as a whole is one of the basic aspects to achieve good results. That culture is connected to the values that live in a company: what has been agreed to be important in the organisation and are those values shared by the employees? A final aspect in this quadrant is relationships: good relationships within teams, between teams and between the company and its customers and suppliers are very important for the proper functioning of a company and its processes. A manager who wants to call himself a leader needs to be able to optimise communication, culture, relationships and values to be successful.

We can conclude that the quotes at the beginning of this chapter are mostly focussed on the following aspects:

o *Behaviour* – Upper right quadrant (Pacific Integral)
o *Relationships* – Lower left quadrant (Michael Hogg)
o *Vision* – Upper left quadrant (David Messick)
o *Group values, beliefs, culture, integrity* – Upper and lower left quadrants (Freud)

The only quadrant that is missing from this list is the lower right one. However, one can imagine that a lot of management activities are already aimed at the areas of organization, change management and economic factors. In some companies this even seems to be the only focus for managers.

So we can already conclude that the various views of leadership put an emphasis on specific aspects from the Integral Model. In the context of this book, I can then make this a short chapter and assume that putting all those views together gives us a full perspective on leadership. Integral leadership, however, consists of more than just showing leadership in all quadrants: it should be an integration of all those aspects into a single vision and acting from that single vision in all quadrants.

The obvious question is then, what is it that creates unity in the various aspects of leadership? That will be the subject of the remaining parts of this chapter.

SO WHAT *IS* LEADERSHIP?

To get to the essence of leadership, look at what all activities that get associated with it have in common: leadership is about connecting to people. Leaders have a way to connect to others; non-leaders fail to connect to others. A leader without followers can hardly be called a leader and therefore leaders need to have found some way to connect to people so they want to follow him.

That was the simple part. Now what is it that leaders have that makes them connect to others? If you ask them, they will not be able to say that they are doing this particular thing or have that specific skill so they easily connect to people. Their ability to connect came naturally or has developed throughout the years. Very few people have found a way to develop their ability to connect to others and actually got there through specific efforts.

The trick is that in order to connect to others, you need to first learn to connect to yourself. This statement is based on a view of the world that says that we are all part of some continuum, like individual waves in the ocean. Individuals, yet part of one larger whole. For now, just accept this as a possible perspective on things, there is no need to get religious about it.

What does connecting to oneself mean? It took me a while to figure that out myself (I am one of those people who learnt it the hard way). In essence, connecting to oneself means getting closer to your thoughts, feelings and actions. Getting closer to your *Self*, if you want it expressed in a more spiritual way. It is about being aware of what you do, think and feel at every moment of the day. This is not easy, for it requires a level of awareness that is extremely high and, in the beginning, pretty tiring. Try to stand still for a moment and realize what is going on: what do you see, what are you touching, what are you hearing, what are you thinking and what are you feeling? Use all your senses and just be aware of what is coming in through them. Now do this for five minutes continuously. Getting tired yet? In any case, it is this awareness or mindfulness, as some people call it, that you need to develop when you want to get closer to who you really are.

Great leaders use that as a starting point – they know themselves through and through, whether they are fully aware of it or not. They use this as a starting point when connecting to others and leading them to wherever they believe the group should go – with positive intentions or negative ones, it doesn't matter. Certain dictators were as much leaders as Martin Luther King was. It's just the intentions that were different.

So once you have, through painful exercise, managed to connect to yourself, you will notice that your interaction with others is changing also. For example, when I started learning to get closer to my feelings, at some point in time I started wondering why people were smiling at me all the time. What I did not realize was that they were actually smiling back at me. I had learnt to express my feelings more effectively and people were reacting to that. Similarly so at other levels: once you become more aware of how you function yourself, you pick up how other people are functioning more easily also.

So, connecting to people requires you to be able to connect to yourself. This is the first step that defines the *attitude* of the manager.

Through the years, it has become my conviction that what is called leadership is in fact determined by attitude as well as *ecology*, which we dealt with before. The next section deals with what this attitude means in practice, indicating that it is closely related to the core of our being and therefore it deserves some closer attention.

Attitude is in my opinion both the most important and the most difficult of skills and abilities that a manager needs to get good results with his team. Attitude is to do with the basic approach of the manager, thus closely related to rapport, as described in a previous chapter. The purpose of the right attitude, however, is to go beyond the levels of rapport described there, beyond having a good understanding at a physical, emotional and rational level between manager and employee. But leadership also goes beyond the aspects from the four quadrants listed in the previous section of this chapter: Behaviour, Relationships, Vision and Group values, beliefs, culture, integrity. It is a step further that is required to get to real leadership, because it is effectively an All-Quadrants-All-Levels (AQAL) aspect of who we are.

I have come to the conclusion that essentially, Leadership originates in the right (personal) attitude which should be complemented by the right ecology. Every other aspect of leadership is embedded in these two. Attitude and ecology are both AQAL phenomena and should therefore be described as such.

We will first have a closer look at attitude: what is it that this attitude involves and how can we put it in practical terms?

I base this practical description of the right attitude of a manager on a number of different sources (see the literature list). In some cases, those sources have described various aspects of leadership; in other cases, they come from a totally different direction, such as methods of self-inquiry or therapy. In any case, they are talking about the same thing: what are the practical aspects of attitude that someone needs to get positive results? Then it does not matter what the field of application is exactly (note that this is similar to how NLP originally started: observing therapists who got positive results in their jobs and from there deriving patterns that determined why they were successful).

Typically (or thankfully!), the sources are not in agreement with each other, even though certain aspects come back in multiple places. It is those aspects that I describe below. Note that these aspects don't only apply to the manager himself, but that the manager as a leader, whether he wants it or not, also has an example function for his employees and for the rest of the company. This specifically applies to attitude. If the manager has the right attitude, the rest of the team will follow.

ATTITUDE IN PRACTICE

What does attitude involve exactly? This varies per person, as everyone has a different way of expressing themselves and showing leadership behaviour. There are no universal leadership traits as such, so you will have to discover and use your own leadership characteristics. What the right attitude does come down to, however, can be described in terms of the four quadrants of the Integral model. Attitude itself lives in the upper left quadrant, but it reflects in leadership traits in the other three quadrants.

I.   **Upper Left**
Development does not always run at the pace or in the direction we would want it to do. In order to be able to coach an employee well, we therefore need to be able to devote a lot of patience to him to give him the time to find his own path. Managers with a more directive style often neglect this and therefore force the work into a direction that is not always the right one for the employee or the company. At the same time, a manager needs to be committed to his job, his team, the people in the team and the goals of the team and

the company. Showing this commitment is important to continuously put the focus on what is important and make that clear to the employees as well.

Try and imagine a state of wonder about where a certain attitude, problem situation or emotion comes from when interacting with employees. This state does not involve wanting to change anything, finding some solution or having an opinion about it, but it is just an objective observation of what is out there. The reality of the moment in this case can be referred to as the truth; that what is happening right now, without being covered in layers of beliefs, values, emotions, etc. Love for the truth is a devotion to finding out what is really going on, what is going on inside the employee and in you as a manager yourself. This is a love that does not originate in the mind, but in the heart and the soul.

Indispensable for the coaching process with people is a curiosity to find out what moves them, what is on their minds and how their work environment can be improved. Helping to look for a solution for their issues is an aspect of the coaching process for which a healthy curiosity is necessary. Love for the truth in its turn is a prerequisite for this type of curiosity.

A manager needs to know *himself* in the first place, meaning he needs a level of self-awareness. This is needed in order to be able to understand the own reactions. When an employee tells the manager about an issue, is the manager's response on the employee's story or is it based on a part of his own history? There is a significant difference between the two. Namely, if the latter is the case, are you as a manager dealing with the issue of the employee or are you dealing with an issue of yourself? When you are dealing with the content of work, as a manager you need to switch of your own filters (i.e. switch off your own Model of the World), because otherwise you are not focussing purely on the employee. This means, that you risk reacting based on your own history and not based on what the employee is going through. For example: an employee comes to you asking for advice on dealing with a colleague who is very aggressive to him and refuses to cooperate. You as a manager may respond to this quickly, because you have dealt with aggressive people all your life and have developed a response to them that you can blindly apply with success. However, this response that you developed may not be appropriate for the employee's particular case, which has a different context, a different person to respond to and the employee is a different person with a different character and a different Model of the World. Knowledge and awareness of yourself is also needed in order to be able to shut off irrelevant thoughts and feelings and as such move your focus back to the employee. Finally, self-awareness simply brings you closer to yourself, so you can feel your response to the other more clearly and hence are able to explain and express it to the other. This brings you closer to a state of pure presence. Presence starts with physical, emotional and mental self-awareness, just to establish who you are. It then is paired with an accurate self-assessment: know what your capabilities are, what your strengths and weaknesses consist of. This then leads to confidence, where you have a strong sense of your own value, your beliefs and your role. Taken together, presence doesn't require you to say much, as this state in itself will already stimulate the employee to open up to you and feel that there is room to speak his mind.

Leadership therefore starts with getting close to yourself, by getting to know yourself, being at ease with who you are and act from that perspective. You need enough knowledge about yourself and your leadership qualities first. It is there where authenticity starts, which is the true core of who we are. This authenticity is also at the basis of building the relationship with others.

Do you know what your *vision* is? Or, let's start with another question: do you know what vision is? Vision in the context of management is the application of your Model of the World to the practice of running a team or a company. How you look at events around you and what these events do with you determine how you respond to them and take action where needed. Your vision should first be understood by yourself, by knowing the aspects that built your Model of the World. Then, you can explain how and why you apply it to practical issues arising in the workplace. You need to share this vision with your employees so they can buy into it in their own way and within their own remit. In that way, your vision will be reflected in your organisation's actions. Ultimately, your vision is what should guide and inspire the members of your organisation.

II. Lower Left

The *communication* of a leader with the right attitude should be confident, but not over-confident. More importantly, the communication should instil confidence into the people addressed, so that they are willing to follow this leader. The leader should also be able to observe things from different *perspectives*: not only the four perspectives from NLP, but also multiple perspectives based on the world views of the people involved in an issue. Communication should be consistent and clear so that the right guidance can be provided to the team and to others.

The right attitude will connect the leader to the people he is working with rather than estrange them. *Connection* starts with rapport, which, in its ultimate form, means that the leader first needs to connect to himself. This connection to the self allows him to transcend his (limited) personal views and instead have an eye for the views of others. Connecting to oneself also allows the manager to let go of his inhibitions, the things that make him hold on to control. Letting go of a high level of control and leaving it to the team to find the right way to handle situations is often an eye-opener for managers. When authenticity, which is part of the upper left quadrant, is present, the connection to other people will follow easily. Authenticity in our attitude is integral to our relationship with others. Leadership is after all about a relationship between the leader and the led.

In a previous chapter, when dealing with setting up emotional rapport, we have dealt with *empathy* already. Being close to oneself and achieving a state of presence will bring us closer to our feelings. Knowledge of your feelings makes it possible to be truly touched by what an employee tells you and to be able to express your being touched to him in return. Being able to do this is an important part of being a coaching manager, because the employee will feel he is being heard and listened to. This level of empathy creates a state of closeness that permits you to intuitively show the right direction to the employee and support him. It will show a level of interest in the person behind the employee, without necessarily having to go into mundane personal details. It is about the connection, not about sharing stories about what you did in the weekend.

Building a team culture is needed to bring the individuals in the team together. The emphasis here needs to be on individual and collective accountability and responsibility where needed and appropriate.

Finally, in this quadrant there is the aspect of cultural and social awareness of the team. In an earlier chapter I mentioned cross-cultural management already: the need to be able to deal with people coming from various cultural backgrounds and making sure they form one team in all their variety. Necessarily, there will be a need to manage conflicts that arise in the team or between team members and other teams. The remedy for conflicts is to build bonds between people: creating relationships that brings the team together and stimulates teamwork and collaboration. Added to this, there is a need to be a champion of change, which starts with believing in the need for the change yourself and then being able to communicate this to the team as well. The team will have an easier time accepting unavoidable changes if their leader actually shows he believes in them as well.

III. Upper Right
The right attitude begets the right behaviour: when you observe someone, his behaviour reflects his attitude. This is in all aspects of external behaviour: posture, look of the eyes, movements, body language, breathing, speaking and, foremost, the actions taken. The actions should be *congruent* with what is said; meaning that the actions should reflect what was promised before and should not be in conflict with them. Leadership means that there is a consistency between what you say and what you do, between words and deeds. The communication from the lower left quadrant should therefore be reflected in the actual behaviour of the leader in the upper right quadrant.

Behaviour is also reflected in the level of self-management a leader has. Self-management is understood to consist of aspects such as self-control, integrity, ecology, conscientiousness, adaptability and initiative. These are all elements of attitude that show up in behaviour and can mostly be easily observed by others. If they are recognised as being present in a leader, the people in the team will more easily accept decisions made by him. If not, followers will not take the leader seriously anymore and eventually leave the team.

IV. Lower Right
Attitude in the lower right quadrant is about the organisation. In the first place, the leader needs to create a view of the *landscape* of what is to be led: the structure of the own organisation, the working

relationships with other organisations, how to act cross-functionally, where the personal influence can be effectively used and where not. It is this organisational landscape that forms the *context* in which the leader functions. His attitude determines his effectiveness working in this context.

There is an element of *coordination* in this quadrant as well: at times it is an act of balancing needs, values and political agendas that is required to keep the business running. This balancing act requires well-developed coordination skills, as if all these elements are hanging from your fingertips and need to be synchronised. The leader's attitude determines whether this is successful or not and whether this ends up being ethically sound or not.

ECOLOGY (REVISITED)

Taken together with attitude, ecology is the other pillar on which the true leader should be leaning. The personal morality is reflected in the leader's attitude, which in turn is to be reflected in the way in which the leader tackles the everyday business needs. Where morality is sound, the business is dealt with ecologically.

Remember what ecology involved: doing no harm to oneself, the other and the environment on a physical, emotional, mental and spiritual level. Business decisions therefore need to take into account the needs of the leader himself, the organisation that is being led, the company as a whole, but also the customers, suppliers, the economy as a whole, society and the environment. This is a great responsibility, which goes beyond what is nowadays referred to as Corporate Social Responsibility (CSR). CSR is too often used as a fashion statement (just as Ethics was ten to fifteen years ago), but only has real value once the needs of all the groups mentioned are met through *personal* moral commitment. A true leader is therefore one who knows how to reflect his personal moral values in his work as a manager and improve the widest ecological environment on a daily basis.

Many years ago, I have made myself notorious with a statement that I made in a team meeting with all my reports present. The discussion was about cooperation within the team and the general working atmosphere. This was all in a time when the company I worked for was going through a series of reorganisation where one department after the other was moved abroad or otherwise eliminated.

In any case, the statement I made there was that I did not consider my colleagues to be friends. This was meant to say that I had a pretty strict division between my working life and my private life. Nevertheless, some people were somewhat shocked at hearing my statement. Especially the foreign people in the team, whose private lives typically depended for a very large part on their relationships with their colleagues, could not understand this. Of course, being a Dutch guy working in Holland, I based my private life mostly on existing relationships with family, friends from school and other people that I had met before even starting to work.

History has proven me wrong. In the past fifteen years, it has happened twice to me that colleagues turned into friends – very close friends indeed. In the first case, this was someone from a different department than mine. In the second instance, though, this was someone who I directly managed. This chapter is about the complications the latter situation brings with it and will, non-surprisingly, become an ethical discussion.

First, however, some martial arts practice.

I have practiced Karate as an adult for three years and got my fair share of bruised ribs, fingers and whatnot in that period, but also belts in various colours (I ended up as a Blue Belt, which is two levels under Black). I had to stop out of sheer lack of time to keep up with the increased intensity of practice at the higher levels, but also because I got issues with the hierarchical nature of the sport (the sheer veneration of the *sampais* and *sensei* was too much for me. Did I already mention before the fact that I have an issue with authority?).

Karate taught me a lot of useful things beyond being able to defend myself physically and mentally, though. One central concept in Karate is that of *ma-ai* (間合い) or the "proper distance". It is explained as the correct distance between yourself and your opponent so that you can most effectively defend yourself or attack the other. This depends on multiple factors, such as your body size, your speed, angle of attack, etc. A proper distance that is too large prevents you from reaching the other, so you will miss contact or will take too long reaching him. A proper distance that is too small prevents you from making the right movements to actually hit the other, because the space is too small to do so. *Ma-ai* is not necessarily the same between opponents: some people are simply taller than others, so the proper distance for the one fighter is different from the proper distance for the other. Being a somewhat smaller person, this was one of the reasons why I tended to collect quite a few injuries during karate practice. Finally, *ma-ai* also refers to a mental distance that is to do with the level of concentration of both opponents.

Translating this back to the subject of this book, the proper distance between a manager and an employee is something we need to consider now. Obviously, we are not referring to a fight between the two nor any physical attacks, but to a decent working relationship where the distance between manager and employee at a professional level is concerned.

What I mean with that proper distance is the following. As a manager you are responsible for many aspects of your employees' working lives, ranging from work assignments, being aware of what they spend their time on, reporting on their activities, career and personal development, coaching, etc. Especially in the latter few items, you need to get closer to the employees as persons, as all sorts of aspects related to their characters and personal history may start playing a role there. Depending on your own character, you will be interested in those aspects in a larger or smaller degree. As you may have gathered by now, with my background I tend to go into somewhat greater depth when it comes to these personal aspects than the average manager. This is not only because it interests me, but also because I feel I have the abilities to help people at a professional level using some of the things I learnt as a counsellor.

However: there's the rub. As a manager, how far can you go into the personal domain of your employees without mixing up professional and personal aspects of this relationship? Even if you have the qualifications, should you deal with personal issues that do not strictly touch on the employee's professional behaviour? So what is the proper distance of a manager to his employees? And, finally, can my employees become my friends?

PROPER DISTANCE IN RELATIONSHIPS

In essence, a relationship is an expression of affection between people. Even a bad relationship is such an expression, albeit of a lack of affection rather than of a presence of affection. As Aristotle already wrote, this affection has a different content depending on the nature of the relationship. Between family members, affection is often much stronger than between friends; a friendly relationship at work has an element of affection, but is of a lesser intensity than affection between good friends. So when the person I already liked as a colleague became my friend, the affection between us had effectively increased to a point beyond the usual level of affection between colleagues.

You might say that this is all very vague, because levels of affection are not clearly measurable. And indeed, these things are up to the people between whom the relationship exists to assess themselves. However, in general terms it can be said that the level or intensity of affection between people determines the type of relationship they are really in. A professional relationship between a manager and an employee can therefore be qualified as having a lower level of affection than a personal relationship between e.g. friends.

A lower level of affection means that the *ma-ai* is larger – there is more of an emotional distance between the two people so that there is less opportunity to reach each other at that level. In my opinion, the proper distance between a manager and his employees should be fairly large: management is not only about pleasant things such as rewarding, coaching and developing people, but sometimes also about corrective actions such as performance improvement plans or harsh decisions, such as having to fire someone. For the latter activities, the proper distance should be large enough to be able to perform them without impacting the relationship.

This is clearly hard to achieve when the affection between manager and employee is larger than that. Simply said, if you cannot fire your employee because the emotional bond is too strong, then you should not be his manager, unless you and your friend have very clear agreements about separating work and private life. And even then I'd find it hard to believe that at an emotional level there would be no conflict between the two of you.

Let's look at things more closely and in the light of the Integral Model, though.

INTEGRAL ETHICS REVISITED – A PERSONAL CASE STUDY

A bit more than a year ago at the time of writing, I hired an engineer into my team who had contacted me a few months earlier, because he had worked in my team before as a contractor, had left a couple of years before and was now interested in joining as a permanent employee. I was happy about that, because I knew him as an excellent engineer and we had had a good working relationship before.

Coincidence had it that he was also the only person I know who shared my birthday and it gradually turned out we had various character traits in common as well (my next book will be called "Management and Astrology"...). In any case, we grew closer and it turned out we were becoming friends.

It was at that point that I started to sense ethical issues, for the reasons that I briefly outlined in the previous section. I was afraid of crossing the boundary between my role as his manager and my role as his friend; on the one hand I wanted to avoid the suspicion of favouritism or even nepotism and on the other hand I did not want our new friendship to be impacted by any management decision I would have to make that might impact him negatively. I therefore transferred him to a different manager in my organisation (I am a Senior Manager, so have managers reporting into me) to create a more proper distance between us. My friend didn't find this very necessary, but my conscience was happier to increase the *ma-ai* at work and decrease the *ma-ai* privately in this way.

A couple of months later, the situation became more interesting. My friend still reported to the other manager and I had to announce workforce reductions in the team (in my company elegantly referred to as "RIF" or "Reduction in Force"). I basically asked the managers reporting to me to nominate people from their teams that would be put on the list of people to be fired – the RIF list. Then I realised that my friend's manager might select my friend to be on the RIF list. And at that point my ethical conscience started acting up, wondering if I should intervene and change that manager's decision if that happened or not.

I decided to discuss it with my friend. I told him in confidence what the situation was and that there was a hypothetical possibility that he might be impacted, even though I thought the chance would be minimal in his case. This of course scared the hell out of him at first. When he got over it, I asked him the question I was having difficulties with, though: should I intervene if for some reason he would end up on the RIF list by vetoing his nomination?

Opinions differed. He had in principle no issues with me intervening to save his job – he quoted experiences working for companies in countries where people coming from the same village consistently protected and supported each other at the cost of others, resulting in true nepotism. Not that he expected something extreme like that from me, but he would obviously like to keep his job and if I could help him doing so it would be greatly appreciated.

I myself still had issues. These were issues related to a central question: can I justify it to myself to save my friend's job if it means that someone else in the team will have to go? I was leaning towards not intervening, but was afraid of the impact that would have on our friendship. We had not discussed situations like this before and were at the beginning of a potentially painful exercise.

Coming home and having told my partner about the situation, he gave me hell. He accused me of unprofessional behaviour by bringing up the question in the first place, given that my friend should not know about the situation at all, as it was strictly confidential. Moreover, he said I should not make a distinction between my friend and other employees, but should decide on layoffs in an objective manner.

Three people, three opinions. It is time to take the Integral Model for Ethics and see if any of us had looked at the full picture.

AQAL ETHICS

Remember the model from chapter 2: there are four quadrants in Ethics: Morality (personal Ethics), Behaviour (the practical expression of Ethics), Ethics (group Ethics) and Laws (Rules). Then there are multiple stages: Egocentric (Me), Ethnocentric (We), World Centric (All of us), and Multi-world Centric (all encompassing).

Let's look at the individual moral levels (Upper Left in the Integral Model) of each of the three people with an opinion here – me, my friend and my partner:

In terms of the display of personal morality (Upper Left), it seems I am somewhere in between the Ethnocentric stage, focussing on the importance of the friendship between me and my friend, and the World Centric stage, when I realise that I should also focus on the general good for my team as a whole. My friend, however, is understandably concerned for his own job, which is at the Egocentric stage. At the same time he values our friendship, which places him also in the ethnocentric stage. Finally, my partner's morality is easier due to the distance he has to the subject: he can view things from the World Centric stage, telling me that I need to focus on the good for the whole team, despite the friendship I have with one team member.

In the Lower Right quadrant, that of rules, the picture looks a bit different: I am breaking the rules of secrecy about the reduction process from an ethnocentric perspective, focussing again on the value of our friendship. Similarly, so, my friend sees this from the same point of view. My partner comes from a World Centric view again, focussing on not breaking the rules to make sure the benefit of team as a whole is kept in mind.

Then there's the Group Ethics (Lower Left): me and my friend are bound by whatever Ethics play a role in our company. In terms of compliance, there is no specific guidance on who to select in case of a reduction in force. Some countries have laws by which you need to remove a function rather than an employee and certain rules of seniority and the likes determine what employee is affected. All that did not apply in this case, though. Nor is there a generic culture of favouritism in the company that would make it more acceptable to treat certain people differently from others. So in this quadrant, there is not much to base ourselves on.

So how are we going to make sense of these perspectives and determine the most appropriate conduct (Upper Right) that I should have shown?

Generally, as Einstein already seems to have said, a problem at a certain level can only be solved when it is looked at from a higher level. So the Egocentric and Ethnocentric levels at which me and my friend perceive the issue are not the levels at which we need to solve this – we need to look at the World Centric level. Or, in short, we need to look at the interest of the team or the company rather than at the interest of me, my friend or our friendship.

Does this mean that my partner is right? If I admit this, he will just be gloating at my expense, so my answer is: yes and no. Yes, because he is taking the easy perspective from a distance where the complexities of having a friendship at work don't play a role. Not being involved in that, he is objectively right saying that I should not have brought this up with my friend in the first place and that I need to keep my hands off a decision that might have been made by my friend's direct manager. And No, because of exactly the same reason: he is not involved in the complexities of a friendship at work, so I need to look at the effects of that separately, which is a thing that can only be done between my friend and me.

SOLVING ISSUES WITH WORKPLACE FRIENDSHIPS

The Ethical challenge then becomes the following: how do you prevent conflicts between the needs of the company and the needs of a friendship? As history has taught me, there is no way to avoid making friends and the office is a very likely place to do so, given that people spend a significant part of their time there. But at the same time, we need to take care to keep seeing things from a higher ethical perspective than one that only involves the two of us.

To bring this into practice and take the world centric approach in all quadrants of the Integral Model we need to go beyond simple compliance with rules and regulations. On the one hand, these apply to the company only and not to the intangible things that exist within a friendship. But also, rules and regulations are at a conformist level, whereas a world centric view is at a higher level than that, allowing us to break the rules if it is for the benefit of us all. Note that "us all" strictly involves more people than just my friend and me, so there is no way that we can break the rules for the benefit of just the two of us.

This then means that our friendship, for as far as it has a role at work, becomes embedded in the team and in the company as a whole. The ethical needs of the team and the company will therefore always take precedence over the needs of our friendship – at work, that is. Practically speaking, the solution becomes tangible now: our friendship becomes split into a private part that is nothing to do with work and may not touch work whatsoever and a part that does touch on our activities in the office and may have an impact on what we do there. This latter part requires some explanation – how is it that a private friendship touches on work? Part of the answer has been given already by the mere existence of the ethical dilemma I described before. Private and professional lives cannot be separated so easily, unless I would be a schizophrenic. Which I believe we are not. Seriously, it cannot be avoided to refer to private things while we are in the office, whether this concerns arranging a get together in the weekend or general interest in each other's private lives. And all that is OK.

What is not OK is the situation where work-related subjects are discussed between friends and where as a result the needs of the friendship get prioritised to the needs of the company. To avoid even getting into these situations, my friend and I therefore needed to determine the boundary between what we can discuss in a certain context and what not. And, to be honest, given that I was hierarchically the more senior person, that responsibility was foremost on my side.

So we came to a detailed agreement.

In the first place, I would not share any sensitive work-related information with him whatsoever, unless he needed to know this for his job. Even if that information would potentially impact him professionally, I would not discuss it with him. My friend, on the other hand, would not have any expectations from me in terms of wanting to be informed about things that were not his business - literally.

Secondly, business decisions that I needed to make that would impact my friend in any way (positively or negatively) would be taken on an objective basis, meaning that I would have to be able to defend my decision to anyone else (including my friend) and not raise any suspicions of nepotism in the case of a decision that would be favourable for my friend. Nor would my friend have any influence on those decisions. Furthermore, in case my business decision would turn out to be unfavourable for him, I would have to explain and he would have to understand the objective reasons why I had made that decision and neither of us would allow this to impact our friendship.

Finally, we would try and avoid speaking about work in a private context. This is unhealthy anyway, but would also avoid possible entanglements of the private and the professional. Again, like with referring to private tings at work, it is unavoidable that privately references are made to colleagues or work situations once in a while, but the context should be clear that business subjects potentially impacting our friendship should not be discussed privately.

EVALUATION – AND THEY WORKED HAPPILY EVER AFTER?

It is about eighteen months later now and a lot has changed. The private and professional relationships went through changes, I have changed position myself, meaning I am not managing my friend anymore, so it is time for an evaluation.

There were some complexities that lived mostly on my side, given that I was the manager and my friend reported to me. The most obvious issue is to do with performance and compensation management. It is easy to be led into temptation and blindly favour your friend. At the same time, this is a fairly easy issue to tackle, because performance and compensation management, if set up correctly, provide you with objective targets to measure someone against. So that's all I needed to do: be objective and I can say that I can now justify every decision I made in this area based on that.

Actual one-to-ones were more subtle: personal interaction has a tendency to stray and I also never really knew how seriously my friend took me as his manager. Here also, it was a matter of staying strictly objective. Whenever I had feedback on his behaviour, for instance, I needed to be sure to have clear examples of what I observed. This is not more than justified, but not everyone asks for examples when being criticised, so it led me to be well-prepared for our meetings. I gradually learnt to stop being too cautious as well and at time we simply agreed to disagree about certain aspects of our work. I generally leave people free to deal with their teams in the way they want, as long as the results and overall approach are aligned with the rest of the organisation.

Being close also had a benefit for me: I could match behaviour in private with behaviour at work. For instance, my friend has a different attitude towards people than I have and therefore approaches people in a different way than I do, both privately and at work. Recognising this as just a character trait in general made me decide to just let him do as he saw fit within the context of my overall approach for the organisation, whereas with other managers reporting to me, I would have intervened more and let them more strictly follow my line. This does not mean I was an "easier" manager for my friend than for others, because we have had good discussions about his approach, it meant that it was easier for me to see why he took a certain approach and what his intentions with it were.

Coming back to the three agreements described in the previous section, I did find the right middle-ground when it came to sharing business information. I knew well what was sensitive, my friend knew well what I could share and what not and also what I could share but was confidential. He was one of the first people to know about my planning to change jobs, which had no further impact on him than getting a new manager, but this had no other ramifications (in fact, my own manager spread the word more quickly than I would have done myself).

As I mentioned before about performance and compensation management, I took my business decisions based on objective criteria. It never came to a point where I had to take decisions that he was very much opposed to or that were perceived as negative for him, which was a blessing in itself.

Thirdly, separating private and professional lives is not straightforward in conversations. This was also due to the fact that we got to know each other at work and therefore the thing that bound us was primarily work. So private conversations would still end up being discussions about work (although these were general rather than detailed manager-employee conversations) and private elements would be discussed at work as well, albeit mostly during breaks.

Reading this back, it sounds as though it was all quite easy to combine. But would I do this again? In a conversation with another friend I made at work (albeit more remotely), I stated that I would not do this again. Being the boss of a close friend does make the relationship different, simply because I need to keep the separation between private and professional constantly in mind. It never became something natural for me, which is more to do with my character and tendency to go into more depth with people in general than with anything else. I still believe a healthy *ma-ai* between a manager and his employees is favourable to the professional relationship. I also learnt that making friends, even very close friends, at work is something I cannot avoid. I prefer not to be their manager at the same time, though.

When I was on vacation a while ago I decided to read a book called *Hardcore Zen* by Brad Warner. I had found it somewhere without knowing what it was really about, so took it with me as light reading material.

It actually turned out to be a very amusing book, dealing with the perspectives of a hardcore punk musician who discovers Zen Buddhism. Half of it dealt with weird stories from the punk music scene, but half of it dealt in a very simple a direct way with some central tenets from Zen. What the book did, though, was to open my eyes (again, I realised, for I had studied Buddhism before) for a very simple truth: *all there is, is the here and now.*

The implications of that statement are that there is no past, because the past has happened, will not come back and cannot be changed anymore. Neither is there a future (and this statement has nothing to do with punk bands!), because the future is still in the making by what we are doing right now. The only thing there is, therefore, is the split second that we call *now*: the now is the time it takes you to read a single word; a moment later it is gone again, turned into the past.

There is only the infinitesimal touch point between past and future that is called "the present" or "now." It is there only where we exist. Our old self of a moment ago is gone already; our new self of a moment from now is not here yet. Ultimately, what we are is the consciousness of a split second, an infinite emptiness filled with a creative force that will shape the next split second and the next and the next.

The awareness or realisation of this fact is in Buddhism called *mindfulness*. I don't claim to be a Buddhist, but I do believe that mindfulness is spot on: we need to be aware of each and every act of ours, moment after moment. We need constantly to be aware of what we feel, think and do *right here* and *right now*. It is about being aware of your mental state, including your intentions, beliefs and motives. This is much harder than it seems - try it for a few minutes, without being distracted by things happening around you, stray thoughts about the future or the past. It's about as hard as meditation is.

Mindfulness leads to a clear comprehension of life: it guides one's actual behaviour to be in line with one's ideals and goals. Once this state is reached, we are acting from our humanity. As a Manager, the greatest compliment I ever received was as follows, "I have rarely worked for someone who involved himself so much in trying to improve things and get them moving, and still remains so humane."

It is that human face of management that I wanted to share with you in this book.

Chapter 1 – Integral Model
Wilber, Ken – A Theory of Everything. Shambhala, 2001.
Wilber, Ken – The Integral Vision. Shambhala, 2007

Chapter 2 – Workplace Ethics
Wilber, Ken et al. - Integral Life Practice (Chapter 10, Integral Ethics). Shambhala, 2008.

Chapter 3 – Integral Performance Management
Maslow, Abraham – A Theory of Human motivation. In: *Psychological Review*, 50(4), 370–96, 1943.

Chapter 4 – Talent Management
McCall Jr, Morgan W. – High Flyers. Harvard Business School Press, 1998.
Roi, Ric - How to select and develop high potential leaders. Right Management/Manpower Group, 2013.

Chapter 5 – The Coaching Manager
Dilts, Robert – Changing Belief Systems with NLP. Meta Press, 1990.
Bandler, Richard et al. – Frogs into Princes: Neuro Linguistic Programming. Real People Press, 1979.
Halliday, Adrian et al - Intercultural Communication. Routledge, 2004.
Hampden-Turner, Charles and Fons Trompenaars - Building Cross-Cultural Competence. Yale University Press, 2000.

Chapter 6 –Leadership
Cameron, E. and Mike Green – Making Sense of Change Management. Kogan Page, 2004.

Hogg, Michael A. – Social Identity and Leadership, in: David M.
Messick and Roderick M. Kramer - The Psychology of Leadership, New
Perspectives and Research. Lawrence Erlbaum Associates, Inc., 2005
Messick, David M. – On the Psychological Exchange between Leaders
and Followers. In: David M. Messick and Roderick M. Kramer - The
Psychology of Leadership, New Perspectives and Research Lawrence
Erlbaum Associates, Inc., 2005
Goethals, George R. – The Psychodynamics of Leadership: Freud's
Insights and their Vicissitudes, In: David M. Messick and Roderick M.
Kramer - The Psychology of Leadership, New Perspectives and
Research. Lawrence Erlbaum Associates, Inc., 2005
Veenbaas, Wibe en Piet Weisfelt - Persoonlijk Leiderschap. Nelissen,
1997
McMichael, James F. - The Spiritual Style of Management - Who is
running this show anyway? Spirit Filled Press, 1996
PriceWaterhouseCoopers - Integral Business,
Integrating sustainability and business strategy. PWC, 2003
Almaas, A.H. – Spacecruiser Inquiry, Shambhala, 2002
Goffee, Rob and Garteh Jones – Why Should Anyone Be Led by You?
Harvard Business School Press, 2006.

Chapter 7 – Boundaries
Aristotle – Ethika Nicomacheia

Chapter 8 – Epilogue
Hardcore Zen: Punk Rock, Monster Movies and the Truth About
Reality - Brad Warner. Wisdom Publications, 2003.

Chapter 1
http://www.kenwilber.com/

Chapter 2 – Workplace Ethics
Durwin Foster and Dr. Timothy G. Black, Counselling Ethics: Enacting an Integral Approach, 2007 (PowerPoint presentation): http://www.bc-cca.ca/2007/Conference%20Papers/foster_Durwin.ppt

Case Studies Business Ethics, Utah Valley State College, 2003: http://www.uvsc.edu/ethics/curriculum/business/

Chris MacDonald, Business Ethics.ca: Cases: http://www.businessethics.ca/cases/

Merck & Co., Our Values and Standards – The Basis of our Success, Code of Conduct: http://www.merck.com/about/conduct.html

Verizon, Your Code of Conduct: https://www22.**verizon**.com/about/careers/**codeofconduct**.html

The Royal Bank of Scotland Group, Integrity Matters: Our Code of Conduct: http://www.rbs.com/crpolicies/

Santa Clara University – Markkula Center for Applied Ethics, Case Studies: http://www.scu.edu/ethics/dialogue/candc/cases/performance.html

Chapter 4 – Talent Management
Talent Management Hierarchy of Needs:
http://admorerecruitment.wordpress.com/2013/03/19/do-todays-candidates-have-a-hierarchy-of-needs/

Oscar Berg: http://www.thecontenteconomy.com/

Chapter 5 – The Coaching Manager
De Helende Olifant: http://www.dehelendeolifant.nl/

Myers-Briggs: http://www.myersbriggs.org/

Enneagram: http://www.enneagram.com/

NLP Meta Programs:
http://www.nlpls.com/articles/metaPrograms.php

European Commission EuroBarometer – Sport and Physical Activity Bulgaria:
http://ec.europa.eu/public_opinion/archives/ebs/ebs_412_fact_bg_en.pdf

Chapter 6 - Leadership
Pacific Integral Leadership: http://www.pacificintegral.com/

Chapter 7 – Setting Boundaries
Skoss, Diane – Maai, http://www.koryu.com/library/dskoss2.html

Hisashi, Noma – The Kendo Reader, Norges Kendôforbund, Norway, http://www.osi.uio.no/kendo/pdf/Noma.pdf (pp. 42-44).

Chapter 8 – Epilogue
Brad Warner: http://hardcorezen.info/

NEURO-LINGUISTIC PROGRAMMING BACKGROUND

Neuro-Linguistic Programming (NLP) was developed in the beginning of the seventies when researchers Richard Bandler and John Grinder observed a number of therapists that were very successful in what they were doing. There were back then already famous names such as Hypnotherapist Milton Erickson, Gestalt Therapist Frits Perls and the family therapist Virginia Satir. To these studies and modelling of these people they added their own background in linguistics, computer science and psychology. In that way, Bandler and Grinder initially created a model of language, the Meta Model. Later they also created a model of human behaviour. These models were published in their first two books, The Structure of Magic (Volumes I and II). Building on this, they and many others (for instance Robert Dilts, Judith DeLozier, Anthony Robbins) added all kinds of elements from psychology, philosophy, system theory and other sciences, which ultimately led to the name Neuro-Linguistic Programming.

THE NAME "NEURO-LINGUISTIC PROGRAMMING"

Neuro-Linguistic Programming is a quite technical expression for a communication model and therefore hard to understand – as such, it fails already in its name to properly communicate its contents. On top of that, the setup of NLP is done in such a technical way, that the description of its principles, methods and procedures seldom leads to a text that can be easily read. An analysis of the name "Neuro-Linguistic Programming" at least indicates what those principles are.

"Neuro" is derived from the Greek word νέυρον for nerve or nervous system. This part of the name indicates that the nervous system is the basis of all human behaviour: how we behave is controlled by the brain. At least, that was the idea of the founders of NLP. In a later chapter, I will show that the relation between behaviour and the neurological structure is a bit more subtle than that. Behaviour is not only determined by little sparks that are sent around our nervous system, but also by the cultural and social environment and the inner experience of humans, for example. However, for the context of classic NLP, it is sufficient to assume that our behaviour is determined by the structure of our nervous system.

"Linguistic" refers to the use of language (Latin: lingua) as an expression of the inner experience of people. That means that we express the things we experience in everyday life in our own particular way by the means of what we say about them. Language functions as a sort of filter through which we express our experience of reality. As a filter, it is essentially an incomplete expression: we omit certain information, whereas other information is stressed. And all of this is done subconsciously. We can however study how someone uses language and in turn, determine how he subconsciously uses these filters to express himself. By consequence, when we understand those filters, we can determine how someone experiences and mentally processes their own reality.

Take for example the following picture:

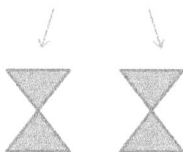

Positive feeling   Negative feeling

"Nice doggie"   "Filthy Animal"

Doggie

Two people who see the same little dog can have a totally different experience of it: this is represented by the top set of filters in the picture. One person likes the dog and has a positive feeling about it; the other doesn't like it and has a negative feeling about it. Those feelings will in turn also be expressed differently: the lower set of filters in the picture. One person with a positive feeling about the dog might say, "What a nice little dog" The other might say, "I get such a happy feeling when I see that dog!" In the same way, the negative feelings can also be expressed in different ways.

NLP typically starts at the other side of the process: we hear what someone is saying and based on that we try to find patterns in his language that indicate how someone's filters are constructed (initially the lower language filters, then the upper filters of experience). When all those filters are clear, we learn to understand the way in which that person experiences the world around him.

Again, this is a particularly limited vision of how physical factors and behaviour are linked, because NLP assumes that all this is determined by the structure of the brain. On the other hand, it is true that clearly discerning these language patterns helps a lot in understanding someone's way of experiencing the world. The rest of this book will go more deeply into this.

Finally, the word "programming" indicates that it is possible to change the behaviour of people by changing the structure and the use of language. So, just like in the example before, we start with the language and we let language do its work to change the subconscious filters in people. For instance, it is a well-known fact that during negotiations, the right use of language can lead to the desired results. Effectively, language influences someone else's behaviour in that way. In the same way, in a therapeutic context the right use of language can change someone's experience of a certain event, by making the experience less traumatic, for example. It should however not be the therapist's intention to use language in such a way that he really shapes or programs the client using language. Language in therapy is only used as a tool to enhance communication and to help the clients discover new insights and perspectives themselves.

After this, some principles of classic NLP are presented, as are examples of their application in Integral Management.

As I indicated before, the expression "Neuro Linguistic Programming" indicates that the neurological structure of man (our brain and central nervous system) can be influenced and even moulded by means of language. This means that through the appropriate use of language and by using the right words, the experience of people in a certain event can be changed. This in particular is what gave NLP a therapeutic application. Beyond that, NLP has also been used for personal development, the coaching of individuals and organisations, sales processes and training management, etc.

NLP has a number of basic principles on the nature and function of man, some of which I will describe in what follows. The principles are important assumptions for the application of NLP in coaching and counselling. That is why I will deal with them specifically in that context.

1. *People have all the resources they need available to them.* With "resource" I mean a skill or ability with which we can react adequately in situations that we have to deal with in our lives. We only react adequately when this capacity is accompanied by the belief that we can apply this capacity in any situation in order to obtain a desired result. For example, if we are insulted by someone, we can react on that in a number of ways: we can get angry and walk away; we can turn silent and start crying; we can say something back that expresses our emotions or even something else. Whether we give any of these reactions depends on a conscious or subconscious belief ("I cannot leave this insult unanswered" or "I'd rather avoid getting into a fight here," for instance). Each reaction gives a different result (the man who insulted us becomes even more insulting or he sees the effect of what his behaviour has provoked in us). Often we react subconsciously. But we can learn to choose the reaction we are giving and in that way we can select the most appropriate or adequate reaction to get the result that we desire. In fact, this principle

indicates that people should be able to react adequately in every situation they encounter. This means that it should be possible for anyone to give the right reaction in a certain situation without being blocked by their own limitations. Limitations can be experiences from the past. Back then, those experiences may have required a certain reaction and can be entrenched in our subconscious minds so that in similar situations nowadays the same reaction is given, whether it be adequate or not. Traumatic experiences can cause these kinds of limitations, but also everyday events that were not experienced as traumatic in the moment they occurred, but were of such a nature that a spontaneous, natural reaction could not or was not allowed to be given. A child that was never allowed to make noise at home may, as an adult, still have to live with certain habits that prevent him from reacting appropriately in a certain situation. The idea behind therapy, amongst other things, is in fact to relieve people from things that block them from reacting adequately in a certain situation. When those barriers are lifted, resources can become available that encourage an appropriate reaction. This principle is applicable to what we consider a "normally developed" person: people with clear mental of physical handicaps obviously don't always have the usual resources available to them.

2. *The map is not the territory.* This most famous of all NLP principles assumes that in the first instance, people make a "map". That is, we create an impression of the world around us based on the information that we receive through our senses. At this point, this is nothing spectacular. But this map is actually a distortion of reality because the information is filtered by all kinds of beliefs and value systems through which a subjective, instead of objective perception of reality is formed. It is the upper set of filters in the picture of the dog above that are responsible for this. This is a process is as though a map (our perception) of a territory (the world around us) is created by a cartographer (ourselves). The map is an image of the territory,

but can never be the same as the territory. First of all, this is because you can never make a map as detailed as the actual territory: the map would have to be the same size as the real territory and that is not practical. Secondly, as the cartographer has a certain impression of the territory (via his senses, beliefs and values) and therefore does not necessarily create an accurate or realistic representation of the territory. The second filter is language (the lower set of filters in the picture). Through language, we can express ourselves about the world in which we live. Language can therefore be viewed as the way in which the world is perceived by the person who uses that language and as a consequence of this, gives information about how the world and what happens in it is interpreted by that person. In other words: how he makes a map of the territory. What needs to be kept in mind, however, is that the map and the territory are not confused, so that the personal interpretation does not turn into the absolute truth about the world or an event in it. In a therapeutic context this means that we as therapists need to realise that the client expresses himself in symbols. Those symbols are models for a reality that only expresses the truth for the client and only represents the truth from the personal perspective of the client. A large part of therapeutic work comes down to getting to know the perspective of the client, and in that way, his view of reality. From that point onwards it can be assessed just how that perspective may actually limit the client's ability to respond in certain situations.

3. *Everybody always makes the best decision possible based on the available information.* This principle means that every reaction given by someone is the correct one for that person in that situation based on the information he has available at that moment. This is even the case if right after that moment, it turns out that the reaction was not the right one. However, nobody makes a wrong choice for himself on purpose. Based on the data they possess about the reality around them, even terrorists or rapists are convinced that what they do is the

right thing to do for them. That positive intention, as it is referred to, may after all consist of satisfying certain needs or striving for a certain ideal. That their actions, in a broader context (i.e. for society or for specific individuals), are not the valid choices is often clear to us bystanders but not necessarily for the person who is making the choice and acts on it. That person has his own view of the world that can keep the wider implications of his behaviour totally out of scope or put it into a totally different context. Looking for the positive intention with the client is an important step in a therapeutic process (and the reason why the positive is always so much stressed in NLP). On the one hand, this is needed in order to obtain an understanding of what motivates the client, but on the other hand, the client also has to realise himself why he exhibits certain behaviour in certain circumstances. Possible feelings of guilt about decisions made in the past can be seen in a different light when it is made clear that the intention of those decisions has been positive from a certain perspective. And that also applies to the acts of others: seeing the positive intention of someone else can take the sting out of a conflict.

4. *There is no failure, there is only feedback.* Resulting from the previous principle, all people make the right choices in all situations, even if the goal is not reached. Not reaching the goal is, as a matter of fact, a result of a lack of knowledge up front. That lack of knowledge becomes immediately clear when the goal is not reached. To illustrate this with a simple example: let's say someone has the intention to hit me (whatever the positive intention of that may be). He will approach me, raise his arm and attack me. However, because I practice karate, I see this happening and can react by stepping backwards to evade his attack and counter him. The goal to hit me is effectively not reached, but the attacker has obtained new information, namely that I can avoid a direct attack. A next time, he will be able to adjust his strategy to have a greater chance of success to be able to hit me. That is why there is no failure, only feedback

that makes it clear that there is not enough information available to make the right choice and succeed. Even if there was enough information available but the skills were not present or not sufficiently developed, it is better to see an unsuccessful outcome as positive feedback from which we can learn, rather than to see it as a failure. This is an important premise for therapy, because in this way the client doesn't need to be disappointed when things do not work out in life. When he learns from his own mistakes he can instead find a stimulus to handle things in a different way next time and succeed.

The following sections deal with varied aspects of NLP, some more technical than others. I am going over those very concisely, because this is not an NLP study book, so I refer the reader to the appendix for references to formal NLP literature, in which things are dealt with in more detail. What I describe next merely serves as necessary background to understand Integral Therapy as I approach it in the rest of this book.

LANGUAGE STRUCTURES; THE META MODEL

As I indicated before, the very first parts of NLP were formed by observing patterns in language, which led to the so-called *Meta model*. This Meta model is a list of eleven patterns used in daily language that are often used subconsciously. Patterns that reoccur with some regularity can indicate what someone's view of the world is made up of. How you use this in practice will become clear in the following example.

AN EXAMPLE FROM THE METAMODEL: TO MUST

Some people often talk in terms of "must", "have to", "ought", "be necessary" and other similar expressions. If these occur regularly and form a pattern, it is called in typical NP-language a "modal operator of necessity". That is just a complex way of saying that the language expresses a certain necessity or obligation. With such people, there can be a trait in their behaviour that can have either in internal or an external source and is, at the very least, worth clarifying. You might confront that person with question like, "What would happen if you don't do so?" or "Who says you should do so?" can bring quite some clarity in the situation.

The Meta model is based on observations and modelling of the hypnotherapist Milton Erickson (and is therefore also called the Erickson-model). This model has divided language in three broad categories of in total eleven language patterns: Deletions, Generalisations and Distortions.

Deletions are patterns in which certain information is not mentioned. Categories of deletions are:
- *Nominalisations*: mentioning a (static) state rather than a (dynamic) process. An example is, "I have a divorce" rather than, "I am going through a divorce."
- *Unspecified verb*: using an abstract verb instead of an explicit description of what is happening. Example: "There is a fight" instead of, "Two people are fighting each other."
- *Missing Reference*: Not stating what you exactly mean. "They have robbed me" – who are "they" exactly?
- *Incomplete comparisons*: using a comparison, but omitting the thing you are comparing something to. For example, "It is better to stop now" – better than what alternative action?

Generalisations are used when things are made more abstract than necessary.
- *Modal Operators*: these are three related patterns in which necessity, possibility or options are expressed. For instance:

- o Necessity: using words like "Must," "Have to," "Obliged," "Ought to," etc. frequently. "We must make our numbers this quarter!"
- o Possibility: using words like "Can," "Possible," frequently. "It is a possibility to try this methodology."
- o Options: using phrases like "Could be," "Should be," "Might," etc. frequently. "We should be in a better shape financially next year."

- *Absolutisms*: using words that show no alternatives: "Everything," "Never," Everyone," "Always." "You are always late!"

Distortions exist in three variations:
- *Mindreading*: filling in the experience of someone else: "You probably won't like this."
- *Lost performatives*: general statements, but without relevance in the situation or actual content. "It is like it is."
- *Wrong cause-effect combinations*: a combinations of cause and effect that cannot be proven or is otherwise invalid. "Whenever it rains I get a headache."

Acknowledging language patterns and using them in daily communication is useful in order to get access to the internal experience and cognitive structure of a colleague. On the other hand, it can be used to detect certain limiting patterns and deal with them. So in the case of someone who frequently uses modal operators of necessity, it is possible that there is an unconscious urge that comes from either outside or inside this person. If this results in a limitation in his ability to function well, it can be useful to check what that urge exactly consists of and find out what its root is.

The Meta Programs in NLP describe a number of patterns that map the way someone functions, acts and perceives in a certain situation. What is it that someone finds important when taking a major decision such as buying a house? Is it the quality of the house itself, the environment, the neighbours or yet something else? A Meta Program indicates this preference we have when taking decisions or in the way we react. In that way there can be a preference to avoid problems, or to face them head-on and find solutions for them. One employee can have a preference to work according to set procedures and the other employee prefers having more freedom in the way he does his job. How someone experiences life and acts on it is determined by these patterns and is subsequently expressed using language. By recognising these patterns, a therapist can gather a wealth of information about the client's functioning. The sixty-odd Meta Programs can be combined in an infinite number of combinations and lead to a structure of the client's personality at a cognitive level. Practically all typologies from other models, such as the Enneagram, can be derived from the NLP Meta Programs.

An example of one of my favourite combinations of Meta Programs (viz. my own) follows below and is commonly known as *perfectionism*.

Perfectionism is a combination of a number of Meta Patterns that are in NLP-language known as follows and will be explained afterwards:

1. The **comparison** between oneself and an ideal image of oneself;
2. A strong **external frame of reference**;
3. A tendency to **mismatch** oneself;
4. **Focussing on the present** and neglecting the past and future.

The combination of all these patterns can lead to someone displaying behaviour that makes him to overly criticise himself and never be content with what he achieves. He will keep striving for the ultimate perfection. The bar is raised constantly and stays unreachable, because the goals moves further and further away. This is a quite common trait in people in the western competitive societies.

The explanation of the NLP Meta Programs above is as follows: a perfectionist is someone who is in a continuous mismatch with himself, so is very critical about himself and focuses on what goals have not been attained yet. An ideal image of himself is created about how he ought to function (the comparison between self and ideal self) and that ideal image is located in the present: he needs to comply with the ideal image right now (focussing on the present). More pressure is applied externally due to an increased sensitivity for what "the others" think of him or what their expectation is (the external frame of reference).

A perfectionist's therapist may propose the following approach based on these patterns. A solution can be found when the ideal image that the client has of himself is placed in the future instead of the present. An ideal indicates after all only a direction to develop in, not a situation that needs to have been attained today. The client should learn to appreciate what he has achieved and who he is right now instead of focussing on what has not been achieved yet and who he wants to be. This does not mean that we should not set goals: on the contrary, we should set goals for the future, not for the present. Looking back at what we have done in the past years, months, weeks and days until today is a positive activity in order to realise what the client has achieved already, because it is probably something to be proud of. Finally, it can be shown that is often more useful to think of what he thinks of a particular situation himself instead of making himself dependent on the expectations and opinions of other people. This will enhance the independence of the client and offers new perspectives, so that he can get a different view on life.

PRIMARY SORTS

Primary Sorts are five categories of language patterns that indicate what people value in specific situations. The patterns indicate in what way someone determines what is important for him. This can be in simple situations, such as work environment, choice of what to eat to more complex cases such as the choice of a life partner or where to live. In the case of choosing a holiday destination, people let themselves be led by various criteria, such as the environment (beach, mountains), travel companions (group, solo or couple travel), what there is to be seen (churches, nature reserves or wine farms), etc. All these variables can be considered concretisations of values, in other words, they are translations of our values (happiness, faith, love, health, etc.) into things you can encounter concretely on your path in life.

The five primary sorts are:

-   **Information**: the focus is on knowledge, the mind, rationality. It is important what can be gathered in terms of new information, what knowledge can be gained.

-   **People**: important is the concern and needs of others, undertaking activities with others; the emphasis is on human contact, feelings and the heart. This can in fact be both in a positive sense (needing a lot of people around you) or in a negative sense (being oversensitive to other people).

- **Activity**: the emphasis is on activity, doing things, getting new experiences. During sports events, you will definitely run into a lot of "activity-sorters."

- **Place:** the focus is on the place where things happen, the qualities of that place and the atmosphere there. This is typical for a choice of a bar or restaurant.

- **Things**: physical items themselves are deemed important. Certain objects (such as art) are appreciated and the quality thereof as well. In an extreme form, this can turn into materialism.

The first three Primary Sorts can be easily derived from how someone speaks: info-sorters frequently use lists, facts and data; People-sorters speak about feelings, emotions, contact, people; Activity-sorters often refer to doing things, action and organisations.

The last two are perhaps harder to discern, because they are more related to the actual content rather than to patterns of language. Place-sorters emphasise the environment; Thing-sorters focus on quality, for instance find brand-names important.

MATCHING AND MISMATCHING

Matching is going along with the other, finding common things, trying to get alignment, among other things by using similar and affirmative language. Mismatching however is not going along with the other, using negations and finding differences between people. A too strong urge to match can lead to a hidden form of self-protection, often due to a negative self-image. A too strong urge of mismatching may lead to obstinacy and be caused by a (perceived) lack of being heard.

DIRECTIONALITY

There is always movement in processes: we are leaving from someplace and we are going to some other place. People often have a preference for a direction: they either focus on leaving the situation they are in (for instance, a problem) or on achieving something (viz. a goal). One can wonder what it is that motivates people most: going away from something or going towards something. These decisions are directly influenced by our values. Someone who mostly aims at achieving a certain state is called a "Towards-type" and someone who mostly tries to distance himself from a certain state is referred to as an "Away-from-type."

If you want to motivate a Towards-type to change his default behaviour, you need to show him that the new direction you want him to go into provides him with some sort of benefit. To motivate an Away-from-type, the person needs to be shown that the new direction avoids something else that is more important to him.

In an ideal situation there would be a balance between Towards and Away-from: you need to know where you are coming from if you want to achieve your goal, but at the same time you can only truly escape your original position if you know where you are fleeing to.

FRAMES OF REFERENCE

Frames of Reference in NLP indicate on what grounds someone determines his decision. What is the criterion that eventually determines what we choose? Do I determine this myself or is it someone or something outside me that determines my choice? There are two possibilities here that are on either end of the spectrum: the internal frame of reference, where the decisive criterion comes from ourselves, namely in the value and beliefs system that we constructed ourselves; and the external frame of reference, meaning the values and beliefs that other people have imposed on us.

Note that these two are not independent of each other. From the moment we were born, we absorb the external frame of reference, because we don't have an internal one to start with. Gradually, this external frame of reference is internalised: we make it our own in the course of our lives, based on other people's opinions and visions, and it then turns into our own internal frame of reference. If all goes well, this process is based on our own life-experience and the internal frame of reference only picks those external elements that are useful for our lives.

This is similar to the model used by Transactional Analysis (TA), where there are a number of roles called Parent, Adult and Child. In TA, the Parent is the part of our personality containing the external frame of reference. The Adult is the part that has filtered the Parent's frame of reference through the experience and emotional responses that the Child has collected. The Adult then contains the internal frame of reference with which we can adequately respond to the situation in which we are.

The aim of development is to live more from our internal frame of reference, so we can have a strong, independent position in society. At the same time, though, we need to be able to use the external one if this is needed. This can be needed in situations where we need to keep the needs of our environment in mind (see also the section about Ecology for more about this). If we want to function well in a society, we need to balance the internal and external frames of reference.

COMPARISONS

People often have the, conscious or unconscious, urge to compare their own functioning and performance with that of others of with and ideal image of themselves. These are comparisons that can tell you something about how someone looks at himself or another person and whether that is in a positive, negative or neutral way. There are six ways of comparisons that can be distinguished.

Comparing oneself to the other. In this case, the won way of functioning is compared to that of someone else in a neutral, objective way. The differences and commonalities are noticed and are not necessarily judged in a positive or negative way.

Comparing oneself with an idealised image of the other. Here, there is also a comparison of the own functioning with that of someone else, but at the same time the other is being idealised, so is seen more (or less) favourably than in reality. Note that idealisation can happen both in a positive way (the other is better, more beautiful, more famous, etc.) and in a negative way (the other is worse, uglier, less interesting, etc.). The main thing to keep in mind, though, is that idealisations are not realistic: the other is seen as better as or worse than the person himself and in that way, the comparison between self and other is not correct anymore. The result is that you end up in a sort of adoration of an ideal image of the other that is not real and hence you start seeing yourself in a non-realistic way instead of who you really are.

Comparing oneself with an idealised image of oneself. IN this comparison, you compare yourself with an image of yourself as you would like to be, but aren't yet. It is a striving for improvement, with the risk that the ideal image is constantly changed and therefore moved to the future continuously. It is frustrating to never be good enough and this can lead, in combination with other meta-patterns, to a negative form of perfectionism.

Comparing the other with an ideal image of the other. This one is a wish to shape someone else (e.g. a partner, child, manager) to an ideal image that you have of them. Obviously, the other can never comply with that image, for it only exists in your mind, but also because the ideal is never going to match the real person. This comparison is often disastrous in relationships: you should realise that you are not married to an ideal image of the other, but with the current other. And there is also the error people make that they can cope with some bad habit of the other, hoping that that habit will eventually disappear. Starting any relationship (including the one between manager and employee) with the intention to "improve" the other's character is a bad basis to start from. Rather, take into account what you don't like in the other and learn to deal with it.

Comparing oneself with oneself. This is a comparison between yourself right now and what you were like earlier. If you do this, you can see how you have changed and what you have achieved; how you have gotten better in what you did and what growth you have gone through. This is a healthy comparison you can do for yourself and the perfect remedy against perfectionism.

Comparing the other to the other. This is the same as the previous comparison, but now applied to the other. Now, you are looking at how the other (partner, child, employee) has changed in time and you can evaluate the growth (or lack of it) of them. Just as how the previous comparison is a remedy against perfectionism, this comparison is a remedy against comparing the other with an ideal image of the other.

In fact, only the last two comparisons of the six are to be considered productive. All other comparisons limit you in your functioning, because the emphasis is too much on what you are not at this moment in time. Instead of that, you better look at the development you have gone through and the benefit you have reaped from it. If there are things you have not achieved yet, there is always the Outcome Frame to set targets in a healthy and realistic way.

Beyond the level of Identity, we arrive in the area of the Transpersonal, which will be dealt with extensively in the last chapter. In this area, we can extend the logical levels in various ways, but for the description in this context, it is sufficient to complete this model with the Mission. Mission is what effectively determines our Identity and is something universal. Mission is in fact the same for every human being, even though the practical application of it, done in terms of Values and Beliefs, Capacities, Behaviour, is different for everyone. Mission is something that convinces us, chooses us and not the other way round: Mission chooses us, we don't choose our Mission. This is true, because Mission is positioned higher in the Logical Levels than Identity, so it transcends us individually. Mission works through us, it is that which inspires us – inspiration can be literally translated as that what puts Spirit into us. It runs through our lives like a thread. It is that thread that we can find by properly observing what we are good at and to see a pattern in it. We will then uncover a thread that leads us to our Mission. For instance, I have discovered that the application of my Mission as a therapist is to enlighten people. This can be explained as making people's lives lighter, but also to coach them to a state of enlightenment, as it is meant spiritually.

The lower levels are things we have and the upper ones are what we are. As we only have those lower four levels, we can also lose them. Practically speaking, this means that we have a certain effect on our environment, but can also lose it by doing something else. We have certain behaviour and can lose it by using different capacities. We have certain capacities and can lose those by applying different values and beliefs. Compare this to one of the principles of NLP that states that everybody has all the resources they need. Finally, we have certain values and beliefs, but can lose them by changing our perspective of the world through our identity. But we can never lose our identity: we are in essence who we are and therefore we can only be our identity, influenced by our Mission, which we also do not have, but which expresses itself through who we are.

Everything we have, we can lose; what we can lose is therefore not who we are. A common mistake is then to identify ourselves with levels that are lower than identity. We can then say that someone "is naughty." Instead of it, we can better say that this person is "showing naughty behaviour" or "behaves in a naughty way." Otherwise we confuse his behaviour with his identity. We are not our behaviour, we have certain behaviour. Similarly, we use expressions related to the effect of our behaviour or the context of it: someone "is British" instead of "has the British nationality." Someone "is a vandal" instead of "displays behaviour with a destructive effect." At the level of capacities, we say that someone "is clumsy" instead of saying, "he doesn't have the skills to do this properly." And it is similarly said that someone "is a liberal" whereas he simply has "liberal convictions."

Confusion of to have and to be at these lower levels can lead to identifications with these levels, which causes, particularly at younger ages, psychological deformations of someone's experience and eventually to complications at a later age. A little child that has been told over and over again that it is "bad" will start to believe in it en will get the belief that is has no choice but to be "bad." Those words can resound until a much later age, through which the experience of this now mature woman is unnecessarily impoverished. However, if the child had been told that it was "behaving badly," it would have had a totally different effect, for what you do can be changed, whereas what you are, is fixed.

As explained before, values exist in a hierarchy, where some values are considered more important than others. Hence, there are "higher" and "lower" values, depending on the personal preferences.

Questions that can be asked to find higher values than the current value are, "Where does it lead to?" or "What does it mean for you." A question to find a lower value is, "What do you need for this?" Values at the same level can be found by asking the question, "What else do you need apart from this to get to <the higher value>?" For example, "What else do you need apart from Freedom (value) in order to get to Independence (higher value)?"

Beliefs can exist at various logical levels. Belief statements at those levels typically begin with the following phrases:

Identity/Role: I am...
Values: I belief...
Capacities: I can...
Emotions: I feel...
Behaviour: I do...

A general formulation of a belief at Identity level is as follows, "If I do this, then I am..." for example, "If I do my best at school, then I am a good student."

Beliefs have a great influence on our lives, because some of them can stimulate us in achieving our goals, but other can limit us in doing so. The latter are referred to as "Limiting Beliefs." Limiting beliefs have the following characteristics:

- Irrational: they are not true in the present (they may have been in the past, though), yet they feel as if they are true.

- Ecologically disturbing, both for the person himself and for the environment (see elsewhere for a full description of Ecology).

- They provide structure and support (and can in a negative sense become a self-fulfilling prophecy), but therefore they are a filter, because there is no possibility for other ways to see reality anymore.

- They have a positive intention, even though the result is a negative influence on life.

- They are deeply anchored in our being: beliefs and certainly limiting beliefs have their roots in our pasts and in that way retain their influence in the present.

STOPPING THINKING

Thinking exists from the level of Values and Beliefs. This is the case, because at that level, we start thinking about what we are doing, what the impact is of what we do on our environment, so about the lower logical levels. Thinking about higher levels is possible too, but only in a way that expresses what we experience there in terms of the lower levels. After all, thinking about your identity is not the same as Identity itself: everything you think of lives on lower levels than Identity according to the hierarchy. Identity is in fact the Thinker himself. Only when we have the choice to think or not to think, we can get to the pure experience of Identity. The condition to get to it is to simply stop thinking and get totally silent inside. Then is when our Identity unveils itself.

RAPPORT AND ECOLOGY

It is no coincidence that the levels of rapport are very much in agreement with the levels of ecology, which I have explained in an earlier chapter. What are depicted in both cases are the subsequent levels of our Being, which have already been described by many of the great world religions and spiritual schools: body, feelings, thoughts and mind. Those are the consecutive and self-embracing levels of our being and those have their influence one the interaction between two human beings and on the context in which this interaction takes place: the ecology. An ecological relationship between two or more people therefore has as its prerequisite that there is rapport between those people. Phrased in a different way it can be said that the proper rapport between people leads to an ecological environment.

Dolf van der Haven (1971) obtained his Master of Science (M.Sc.) in Geophysics in 1995 at Utrecht University and after that started working in the ICT Industry. In the more than fifteen years that he has been working in that environment, he has had various technical, managerial and consultancy positions in large ICT companies.

In parallel to this, he studied Neuro-Linguistic Programming and Counselling with Chris van de Velde and Eric Schneider at the Dutch Academy for Psychotherapy in Amsterdam, where he graduated in 2005. Dolf has studied many subjects over the years in areas such as psychology, philosophy, languages, western and non-western cultures, religions and spirituality.

He founded his company for coaching and counselling (Integral Coaching & Counselling Van der Haven) in 2005 and co-founded Powerful Answers, an international IT Service Management consultancy, in 2014.

Dolf published his first book, *The Healing Elephant,* in 2008. He is married and lives with his partner and an ever-increasing number of chickens and ducks in Groenekan, The Netherlands.

www.ingramcontent.com/pod-product-compliance
Lightning Source LLC
Chambersburg PA
CBHW072351200326
41519CB00015B/3729